What Readers Are Saying About
New Programmer's Survival Manual

I love the pragmatic tone and content.

➤ **Bob Martin**
President, Object Mentor, Inc., and author of *The Clean Coder*

An excellent overview of the "big picture" and the many facets of software development that a lot of new developers lack. A great primer for starting an exciting career in software development.

➤ **Andy Keffalas**
Software engineer and team lead

A funny, honest, inside look at the ever-growing, ever-changing industry of writing code. If you just got handed your CS degree, this book is a must-have.

➤ **Sam Rose**
Computer science student, University of Glamorgan

This book has everything I should have sought out to learn when I started in the industry. A must-read for new developers and a good read for everyone in the industry.

➤ **Chad Dumler-Montplaisir**
Software developer

New Programmer's Survival Manual

Navigate Your Workplace, Cube Farm, or Startup

Josh Carter

The Pragmatic Bookshelf

Dallas, Texas • Raleigh, North Carolina

Pragmatic Bookshelf

Many of the designations used by manufacturers and sellers to distinguish their products are claimed as trademarks. Where those designations appear in this book, and The Pragmatic Programmers, LLC was aware of a trademark claim, the designations have been printed in initial capital letters or in all capitals. The Pragmatic Starter Kit, The Pragmatic Programmer, Pragmatic Programming, Pragmatic Bookshelf, PragProg and the linking *g* device are trademarks of The Pragmatic Programmers, LLC.

Every precaution was taken in the preparation of this book. However, the publisher assumes no responsibility for errors or omissions, or for damages that may result from the use of information (including program listings) contained herein.

Our Pragmatic courses, workshops, and other products can help you and your team create better software and have more fun. For more information, as well as the latest Pragmatic titles, please visit us at *http://pragprog.com*.

The team that produced this book includes:

Susannah Pfalzer (editor)
Potomac Indexing, LLC (indexer)
Kim Wimpsett (copyeditor)
David J Kelly (typesetter)
Janet Furlow (producer)
Juliet Benda (rights)
Ellie Callahan (support)

Printed in the United States of America.
ISBN-13: 978-1-934356-81-4
Printed on acid-free paper.
Book version: P1.0—November 2011

For Daria and Genevieve.

Contents

Part II — People Skills

Part III — The Corporate World

Part IV — Looking Forward

Acknowledgments

First, I must thank my ever-patient editor, Susannah Davidson Pfalzer. This book couldn't have happened without her clear-minded guidance, words of encouragement, and occasional swift kick in the rear to keep me going. Susannah, thank you so much for helping this first-time author bring a book to life.

Next, numerous reviewers ranging from new programmers to industry pros provided tremendous help. They read (or should I say, *endured*) early drafts of this book and offered their own viewpoints, expertise, and corrections. I'd like to thank Daniel Bretoi, Bob Cochran, Russell Champoux, Javier Collado, Geoff Drake, Chad Dumler-Montplaisir, Kevin Gisi, Brian Hogan, Andy Keffalas, Steve Klabnik, Robert C. Martin, Rajesh Pillai, Antonio Gomes Rodrigues, Sam Rose, Brian Schau, Julian Schrittwieser, Tibor Simic, Jen Spinney, Stefan Turalski, Juho Vepsäläinen, Nick Watts, and Chris Wright. You have all made this book far, far better with your diligent and thorough reviews. I—and every reader of this book—appreciate your work.

From the beginning, several friends and co-workers allowed me to pester them over and over again for advice, including Jeb Bolding, Mark "The Red" Harlan, Scott Knaster, David Olson, Rich Rector, and Zz Zimmerman. I truly appreciate your patience.

Finally, an extra-special thanks for my two biggest fans. My daughter, Genevieve, gave me grace many, many evenings as I needed to duck away and write. And my wife, Daria, not only gave me time to write, but she was the first to buy and read the beta version of the book—in one sitting, no less, starting at ten at night. She offered her thoughts and perspective since this book was just an idea I was pondering over the dinner table. And she provided her support and encouragement through the whole process.

Daria and Genevieve, I couldn't have done it without you. Thank you from the bottom of my heart.

Introduction

It's day one on the job. You have programming chops, you've landed the job, you're sitting at your workstation...now what? Before you, a new jungle awaits:

- Programming at industry scale, with code bases measured in thousands (or hundreds of thousands) of lines of code. How do you get your bearings and start contributing quickly?

- Navigating an organization containing programmers but also people in many, many other roles. When you need guidance on a product feature, who do you ask?

- Building your portfolio of achievements each year. When performance reviews lurk on the horizon, do you know what your boss is looking for and how you'll be judged?

...and so much more. Your programming skills are only one part of what you'll need in these first years on the job.

The lucky among us have guides who already know the landscape. This book is a *virtual guide*. It'll get you oriented, point out the mountains and canyons ahead, and also save you from some nasty pitfalls.

Where I'm Coming From

You may find some similarity between your experience and where I stood in college in 1995: I started on a traditional path, a computer science and electrical engineering program at Duke University. I went to my advisor, asking about classes that would best prepare me for working in industry. He was a smart guy—a Rhodes scholar and rising star in the engineering school—and he responded, "I have no idea. I've never worked a day in industry in my life."

I was more than a little disillusioned. I wanted to build real, shipping products—not write research papers. So, that summer I managed to get my foot in the door at one of the hottest start-ups in Silicon Valley, General Magic. It was founded by some of the same guys who created the original Macintosh computer, Andy Hertzfeld and Bill Atkinson. My peers included some of the top players from Apple's System 7 (operating system) team and the guy who would later found eBay.

I learned more about programming in my two-month internship than I could have learned in two years of school. I called Duke and said I wasn't coming back. And so my wild ride in industry began.

And Now About You

Readers of this book will fall into a few broad categories:

- College students and recent graduates taking computer science classes and wondering, "Is this what programming is like in the real world?" (Short answer: no.)

- Professionals from other backgrounds who got into programming as a hobby or side job, now wanting to take it on full-time.

- Others who are considering a job in programming but want the skinny on what the books and classes aren't telling them.

Regardless of path, here you are: it's time to pay the bills with code. There are plenty of books out there on the code part. There's not so much on *everything else* that goes with the job—and that's where this book comes in.

For the professionals coming from other fields, some sections won't apply as much to you—you don't need *me* to tell you what marketing does if your background is marketing. However, you will still benefit from details about how things run within the engineering department and how code evolves from concept to release.

Structure of This Book

This book is written in small mini-chapters, called *tips*, that are designed to address a single topic within a few pages. Some are longer by necessity. Related tips are close together, but you can read them in any order. If you're going for the big picture, go ahead and read it from cover to cover. But feel free to flip around—when tips need to reference each other, that's stated explicitly in the text.

We start close to the code: Chapter 1, *Program for Production*, on page 3 starts from your programming talent and gives you guidance on making it production-ready. Nobody wants to ship buggy code, but it's especially challenging on industrial-scale projects to ensure that your code is correct and well-tested.

Next, Chapter 2, *Get Your Tools in Order*, on page 59 helps with your workflow. You'll need to coordinate with others, automate builds, and learn new technologies as you go. Plus, you'll need to hammer out a *ton* of code. It pays to invest in your tools up front.

Then we get into the squishier side of things. The one manager you'll have throughout your life is *you*, and Chapter 3, *Manage Thy Self*, on page 101 gets you started on issues such as stress management and job performance.

No programmer is an island, so Chapter 4, *Teamwork*, on page 133 focuses on working with others. Don't discount people skills—true, you were hired to be good at computers, but industry is a team sport.

Then we get to the bigger picture. Chapter 5, *Inside the Company*, on page 155 considers all the moving pieces that make up a typical high-tech company and your part within the whole. It ultimately tries to answer, "What do all these people do all day?"

Closer to home is the business of software. Chapter 6, *Mind Your Business*, on page 181 gets into who's paying your paycheck and why, the life cycle of a software project, and how your day-to-day programming changes with that life cycle.

Finally, Chapter 7, *Kaizen*, on page 211 looks forward. The Japanese *Kaizen* is a philosophy of continuous improvement, and I hope to see you on that path before we part ways.

Conventions Used in This Book

I often use the Ruby programming language in tips that have example code. I chose Ruby simply because it's concise and easy to read. Don't worry if you don't know Ruby; the intent of the code should be self-evident. The examples are intended to demonstrate bigger-picture principles that may apply to any programming language.

Throughout the book you'll encounter sidebars titled *industry perspective*. These are voices from industry pros: programmers and managers who have been down this road before. Each contributor has decades of experience, so consider their advice carefully.

White Belt to Black Belt (and Back)

Throughout the book I use the notion of martial arts belts to signify when you'll need to apply a certain tip. The coloring of belts has a story behind it that is helpful beyond the martial arts. When a student begins, she starts with a white belt, signifying innocence. White-belt tips, likewise, apply from the very beginning.

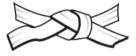

Over years of practice, her belt becomes soiled. The brown belt is an intermediate step where the belt is, frankly, dirty. (We modern wimps just buy a new belt that's colored brown.) For this book, I expect brown-belt topics to become relevant between years two and five.

As the artist practices further, her belt becomes darker and darker until it's black. At this point, she dons the title *master*. For the book I draw the line rather early, where black-belt topics may apply around year five and onward. In real life, true mastery begins more around year ten.

What happens as the new master continues to use her belt? It becomes frayed and bleached from sunlight...it starts to become white again. The masters of old discovered something about expertise that psychologists have only recently studied: you need to get to a certain threshold before you can *know* what you *don't know*. And then you begin your learning anew.

Online Resources

This book's web page is located here:

http://pragprog.com/titles/jcdeg

From here you can participate in a discussion forum with me and other readers, check the errata for any bugs, and report any new bugs you discover.

Onward

Enough chatter about the book. You're sitting at your workstation wondering, "Now what?" And your boss is wondering why you're not working yet. So, let's get going!

Part I

Professional Programming

CHAPTER 1

Program for Production

When you program for fun, it's easy to skimp on things such as handling edge cases, error reporting, and so forth. It's a pain. But when you *program for production*—not to mention a paycheck—you can't take the shortcuts.

Production-quality code seems like a straightforward goal, but our industry has had a heck of a time figuring out how to get it right. Windows 95, for example, had a bug that would hang the OS after 49.7 days of continuous operation—which wouldn't be especially surprising except that this bug took *four years* to discover because other bugs would crash Windows 95 long before 49.7 days could pass.[1]

You can take one of two approaches to quality: build it in from the beginning, or beat it in afterward. The former approach requires a lot of discipline in your day-to-day coding. The latter requires a lot of testing and, in the end, a lot of work *after* you thought you were done.

Beat-it-in-afterward is how it's usually done. It's implicit in the waterfall development method that dominates industry: specify, design, build, test. Test comes last. The product goes to the test department and blows up quickly. It goes back to engineering, you fix bugs, you give another version to the test department, that blows up in some other way, and so it goes back and forth for many months (even years).

Much of this chapter's focus is on build-it-in techniques because that's how you build a product that you can have

---

1. http://support.microsoft.com/kb/216641

confidence in, add features to, and maintain for years. Of course, building production-quality software is a topic that spans more than one book, and its scope is much larger than testing. This discussion, however, is limited to things you can do *right now* to improve the quality of your code:

- Before getting into specific practices, we start with Tip 1, *Beat Up Your Code*, on page 6 to get you into the right mind-set.

- Next, in Tip 2, *Insist on Correctness*, on page 11, we focus on verifying that your code does what it should.

- You can also go the other way around; in Tip 3, *Design with Tests*, on page 21, we look at starting from tests and using those tests to drive your design.

- Very soon you'll be swimming in a huge code base. Tip 4, *Tame Complexity*, on page 27 deals specifically with the sheer mass of production-sized software projects.

- Tip 5, *Fail Gracefully*, on page 35 takes us far off the happy path, where your code needs to cope with problems outside its control.

- Just when things get really gnarly, we take a short breather: Tip 6, *Be Stylish*, on page 41 helps you keep your code pretty—and that helps more than you'd imagine over the long haul.

- Back to the hard stuff. Tip 7, *Improve Legacy Code*, on page 48 deals with code you've inherited from your predecessors.

- Finally, in Tip 8, *Review Code Early and Often*, on page 53 you'll work with your team to ensure your code is ready to deploy.

A Note on What's Not Here

There are other aspects to production-worthiness I don't have space to address, and within many industries there are domain-specific standards you need to meet, too. The following are examples:

- Defensive programming against malicious code, network activity, and other security concerns

- Protection of users' data from hardware and systems failure, software bugs, and security breaches

- Deployment and scale-out performance of software put under great load

- ...and so forth

Consult a senior programmer for advice: beyond writing code that works—all the time, every time—what else does it take for your code to pass muster?

Tip 1

Beat Up Your Code

 [*White Belt*]   As soon as you write production code, you need to prove it can take a beating.

You might think that writing solid code is an obvious job requirement. It's not like the job post said "Wanted: programmer with good attitude, team player, foosball skills. Optional: writes solid code." Yet so many programs have bugs. What gives?

Before we get into detailed discussions of day-to-day practices for assuring code quality, let's discuss what it means to write solid code. It's not just a list of practices; it's a mindset. You must *beat up* your code, and the product as a whole, before it goes out to customers.

The customer, after all, will beat up your product. They'll use it in ways you don't anticipate. They'll use it for extended periods of time. They'll use it in environments you didn't test in. The question you must consider is this: how many bugs do you want your customer to find?

The more *you* beat up your code *right now*, before it gets into customers' hands, the more bugs you'll flush out, and the fewer you'll leave for the customer.

Forms of Quality Assurance

Although much of this chapter focuses on code-level quality and unit testing, assuring product quality is a much larger topic. Let's consider what your product will need to endure.

Code Review

The first obvious, simple way to assure code quality is to have another programmer read it. It doesn't need to be a fancy review, either—even pair programming is a form of real-time code review. Teams will use code reviews to catch bugs, enforce coding style and standards, and also spread knowledge among team members. We'll discuss code reviews in Tip 8, *Review Code Early and Often*, on page 53.

Unit Tests

As you're building the business logic of your application, class by class and method by method, there's no better way to verify your code than with unit tests. These innards-level tests are designed to verify bits of logic in isolation. We'll discuss them in Tip 2, *Insist on Correctness*, on page 11 and Tip 3, *Design with Tests*, on page 21.

Acceptance Tests

Where unit tests view the product from the inside out, *acceptance tests* are designed to simulate real-world users as they interact with the system. Ideally, they are automated and written as a narrative of sorts. For example, an automated bank teller application could have an acceptance story like this: given that I have $0 in my checking account, when I go to the ATM and select "Withdrawal" from "Checking Account," then I should see "Sorry, you're eating Ramen for dinner tonight."

Shakespeare it is not, but these tests exercise the whole system from the user interface down to business logic. Whether they're automated or performed by people, your company needs to know—before any customers play with it—that all system components are cooperating like they should.

Load Testing

Load tests put the product under realistic stress and measure its responsiveness. A website, for example, may need to render a given page in 100 milliseconds when there are a million records in the database. These tests will uncover correct-but-bad behavior, such as code that scales exponentially when it needs to scale linearly.

Directed Exploratory Testing

Acceptance tests cover all of the product's behavior that was specified, perhaps via a product requirements document or meetings. Yet programmers can usually think of ways to break it—there are always dark corners that the specification

Just How Full Are "Full System" Tests?

I spent several years writing control software for industrial robots. Unit tests would simulate the motor movements so I could test the business logic on a workstation. Full-system tests, of course, needed to run on real robots.

The great thing about robots is you can *see* your code at work. The not-so-great thing is you can see (and hear and sometimes smell) your code fail. But more importantly, robots are not a perfect environment. Each robot is different—it's a combination of thousands of mechanical and electrical parts, each with some variation. Therefore, it's essential to test with multiple robots.

The same is true of more traditional systems: vendor software can crash, networks have latency, hard disks can barf up bad data. Your company's test lab should simulate these less-ideal environments, because ultimately your product will encounter them in customers' hands.

overlooks. Directed exploratory testing ferrets out those corner cases.

This testing is often performed by a human, perhaps the programmers themselves, to explore and discover problems. Past the initial exploration, however, any useful tests are added to the acceptance test suite.

There are specialized variations on this theme, such as a security audit. In those cases, a specialized tester uses their domain expertise (and perhaps code review) to direct their testing.

Agency Testing

Hardware products need various agency certifications: the FCC measures electromagnetic emissions to ensure the product doesn't create radio interference; Underwriter's Laboratories (UL) looks at what happens when you set the product on fire or lick its battery terminals. These tests are run before a new product is launched and any time a hardware change could affect the certification.

Environmental Testing

Hardware products also need to be pushed to extremes in operating temperature and humidity. These are tested with

White Box, Black Box

You'll hear the terms *white-box* and *black-box* testing. In white-box testing, you get to look inside the program and see whether everything is working right. Unit tests are a good example.

Black-box testing, on the other hand, looks at the product as the customer would see it; what goes on inside isn't relevant, only that the product does the right thing on the outside. Acceptance and load tests are forms of black-box testing.

an environmental chamber that controls both factors; it goes to each of the four extremes while the product is operating inside.

Compatibility Testing

When products need to interoperate with other products—for example, a word processing program needs to exchange documents with other word processors—these compatibility claims need to be verified on a regular basis. They may run against a corpus of saved documents or in real time with your product connected to other products.

Longevity Testing

You'll notice that most of the tests mentioned here are run as often and as quickly as possible. Some bugs, however, show up only after extended use. Our 49.7-day bug is a good example—that comes from a 32-bit counter that increments every millisecond, and after 49.7 days it rolls over from its maximum value back to zero.[2] You won't be able to find a bug like that unless you run tests for extended durations.

Beta Test

Here's where the product goes out to real customers—but they're customers who know what they're getting into, and they've agreed to submit reports if they find problems. The purpose of a beta test is exactly what we discussed at the beginning of this tip: the beta tester will use the product in ways you don't anticipate, test it for extended periods of time, and test it in environments you didn't test in.

2.　$2^{32} = 4,294,967,296$ milliseconds = 49.7 days, assuming an unsigned counter. See GetTickCount() on Windows as an example.

Ongoing Testing

Your company may continue to test after a product ships. For hardware products in particular, it's useful to pull a unit off the manufacturing line once in a while and verify that it works. These ongoing tests are designed to capture problems due to variations in parts or assembly process.

Practices vs. Mind-Set

Your team may have practices like "all code must have unit tests" or "all code must be reviewed before checking in." But none of these practices will guarantee rock-solid code. Think about what you'd do if there were zero quality practices at your company—how would *you* beat up your code to make sure it's solid?

This is the mind-set you need to establish before going further. Commit to solid code. The quality practices are just a means to an end—the ultimate judge will be the product's reliability in the hands of your customers. Do you want to have your name associated with a product that hit the market as a buggy piece of junk? No, of course not.

Actions

- Of all the forms of testing mentioned earlier, which of these does your company use? Find the unit tests in the source code, ask the test department for the acceptance test plan, and ask how beta tests are done and where that feedback goes. Also ask a senior engineer's opinion: is this enough to ensure a smooth experience for the customer?

- Spend some time doing directed exploratory testing, even if your "direction" is somewhat vague. Really *use* the product to see whether you can break it. If you can, file bug reports accordingly.

Insist on Correctness

[*White Belt*] These considerations are essential to your coding from day one.

In toy programs it's easy to tell the difference between correct and incorrect. Does factorial(n) return the correct number? That's easy to check: one number goes in, and another number comes out. But in big programs, there are potentially many inputs—not just function parameters, but also state within the system—and many outputs or other side effects. That's not so easy to check.

Isolation and Side Effects

Textbooks love to use math problems for programming examples, partly because computers are good at math, but mostly because it's easy to reason about numbers in isolation. You can call factorial(5) all day long, and it'll return the same thing. Network connections, files on disk, or (especially) users have a nasty habit of not being so predictable.

When a function changes something outside its local variables—for example, it writes data to a file or a network socket—it's said to have *side effects*. The opposite, a *pure* function, always returns the same thing when given the same arguments and does not change any outside state. Obviously, pure functions are a lot easier to test than functions with side effects.

Most programs have a mix of pure and impure code; however, not many programmers think about which parts are which. You might see something like this:

```ruby
ReadStudentGrades.rb
def self.import_csv(filename)
  File.open(filename) do |file|
    file.each_line do |line|
      name, grade = line.split(',')
```

```
      # Convert numeric grade to letter grade
      grade = case grade.to_i
        when 90..100 then 'A'
        when 80..89 then 'B'
        when 70..79 then 'C'
        when 60..69 then 'D'
        else 'F'
      end

      Student.add_to_database(name, grade)
    end
  end
end
```

This function is doing three things: reading lines from a file (impure), doing some analysis (pure), and updating a global data structure (impure). As this is written, you can't easily test any one piece.

Said this way, it's obvious that each task should be isolated so it can be tested separately. We'll discuss the file part shortly in *Interactions*, on page 13. Let's pull the analysis bit into its own method:

ReadStudentGrades2.rb
```
def self.numeric_to_letter_grade(numeric)
  case numeric
    when 90..100 then 'A'
    when 80..89 then 'B'
    when 70..79 then 'C'
    when 60..69 then 'D'
    when 0..59 then 'F'
    else raise ArgumentError.new(
      "#{numeric} is not a valid grade")
  end
end
```

Now numeric_to_letter_grade() is a pure function that's easy to test in isolation:

ReadStudentGrades2.rb
```
def test_convert_numeric_to_letter_grade
  assert_equal 'A',
    Student.numeric_to_letter_grade(100)
  assert_equal 'B',
    Student.numeric_to_letter_grade(85)
  assert_equal 'F',
    Student.numeric_to_letter_grade(50)
  assert_equal 'F',
    Student.numeric_to_letter_grade(0)
end
```

```
def test_raise_on_invalid_input
  assert_raise(ArgumentError) do
    Student.numeric_to_letter_grade(-1)
  end

  assert_raise(ArgumentError) do
    Student.numeric_to_letter_grade("foo")
  end

  assert_raise(ArgumentError) do
    Student.numeric_to_letter_grade(nil)
  end
end
```

This example may be trivial, but what happens when the business logic is complex and it's buried in a function that has five different side effects? (Answer: it doesn't get tested very well.) Teasing apart the knots of pure and impure code can help you test correctness both for new code and when maintaining legacy code.

Interactions

Now what about those side effects? It's a huge pain to augment your code with constructs like "If in test mode, don't actually connect to the database...." Instead, most languages have a mechanism for creating *test doubles* that take the place of the resource your function wants to use.

Let's say we rewrote the previous example so that import_csv() handles only the file processing and passes the rest of the work off to Student.new():

```
ReadStudentGrades3.rb
def self.import_csv(filename)
  file = File.open(filename) do |file|
    file.each_line do |line|
      name, grade = line.split(',')

      Student.new(name, grade.to_i)
    end
  end
end
```

What we need is a test double for the file, something that will intercept the call to File.open() and yield some canned data. We need the same for Student.new(), ideally intercepting the call in a way that verifies the data passed into it.

Ruby's Mocha framework allows us to do exactly this:

ReadStudentGrades3.rb
```ruby
def test_import_from_csv
  File.expects(:open).yields('Alice,99')
  Student.expects(:new).with('Alice', 99)

  Student.import_csv(nil)
end
```

This illustrates two points about testing interactions between methods:

- Unit tests must not pollute the state of the system by leaving stale file handles around, objects in a database, or other cruft. A framework for test doubles should let you intercept these.

- This kind of test double is known as a *mock object*, which verifies expectations you program into it. In this example, if Student.new() was not called or was called with different parameters than we specified in the test, Mocha would fail the test.

Of course, Ruby and Mocha make the problem *too* easy. What about those of us who suffer with million-line C programs? Even C can be instrumented with test doubles, but it takes more effort.

You can generalize the problem to this: how do you replace one set of functions at runtime with another set of functions? (If you're nerdy enough to think "That sounds like a dynamic dispatch table," you're right.) Sticking with the example of opening and reading a file, here's one approach:

TestDoubles.c
```c
struct fileops {
    FILE* (*fopen)
        (const char *path,
         const char *mode);
    size_t (*fread)
        (void       *ptr,
         size_t      size,
         size_t      nitems,
         FILE        *stream);
    // ...
};

FILE*
stub_fopen(const char *path, const char *mode)
{
    // Just return fake file pointer
```

```
    return (FILE*) 0x12345678;
}

// ...

struct fileops real_fileops = {
    .fopen = fopen
};

struct fileops stub_fileops = {
    .fopen = stub_fopen
};
```

The fileops structure has pointers to functions that match the standard C library API. In the case of the real_fileops structure, we fill in these pointers with the real functions. In the case of stub_fileops, they point to our own stubbed-out versions. Using the structure isn't much different from just calling a function:

TestDoubles.c
```
// Assume that ops is a function parameter or global
struct fileops *ops;
ops = &stub_fileops;

FILE* file = (*ops->fopen)("foo", "r");
// ...
```

Now the program can flip between "real mode" and "test mode" by just reassigning a pointer.

Type Systems

When you refer to something like 42 in code, is that a number, a string, or what? If you have a function like factorial(n), what kind of thing is supposed to go into it, and what's supposed to come out? The *type* of elements, functions, and expressions is very important. How a language deals with types is called its *type system*.

The type system can be an important tool for writing correct programs. For example, in Java you could write a method like this:

```
public long factorial(long n) {
  // ...
}
```

In this case, both the reader (you) and the compiler can easily deduce that factorial() should take a number and return a

The $60 Million Break Statement

On January 15, 1990, AT&T's phone network was humming along just fine. Until, that is, at 2:25 p.m. when a phone switch performed a self-test operation and reset itself. Switches don't reset often, but the network can handle it, and the switch takes a mere four seconds to reset and resume normal operation. Only this time, *other* switches started to reset, too, and within seconds all 114 of AT&T's backbone switches were endlessly resetting themselves. The mighty AT&T phone system ground to a halt.

It turns out that when the first switch reset itself, it sent a message to neighboring switches saying it was resuming normal operation. The exchange of messages caused the neighboring switches to crash. They, in turn, automatically reset and sent messages to *their* neighbors about resuming operation, and so on…thus creating an endless reset/resume/reset cycle.

It took AT&T engineers nine hours to get the phone system working again. It's estimated the outage cost AT&T $60 million in dropped calls, and it's impossible to gauge the economic damage to others who relied on their phones to do business.[a]

What was the cause of the problem? A mistaken break statement. In C, someone had written this:

```
if (condition) {
    // do stuff...
}
else {
    break;
}
```

On the surface, the code reads like "If the condition is true, then do stuff; else, do nothing." But in C, break does not break out of an if() statement; it breaks out of other blocks like while() or switch(). What happened is that the break broke out of an enclosing block much too early, corrupted a data structure, and caused the phone switch to reset. Because all the phone switches were running the same software and this bug was in the code that handled messages from peers about a reset recovery, the failure cascaded back and forth through the whole network.

---

a.   http://users.csc.calpoly.edu/~jdalbey/SWE/Papers/att_collapse.html

number. Java is *statically typed* because it checks types when code is compiled. Trying to pass in a string simply won't compile.

Compare this with Ruby:

```
def factorial(n)
  # ...
end
```

What is acceptable input to this method? You can't tell just by looking at the signature. Ruby is *dynamically typed* because it waits until runtime to verify types. This gives you tremendous flexibility but also means that some failures that would be caught at compile time won't be caught until runtime.

Both approaches to types have their pros and cons, but for the purposes of correctness, keep in mind the following:

- Static types help to communicate the proper use of functions and provide some safety from abuse. If your factorial function takes a long and returns a long, the compiler won't let you pass it a string instead. However, it's not a magic bullet: if you call factorial(-1), the type system won't complain, so the failure will happen at runtime.

- To make good use of a static type system, you have to play by its rules. A common example is the use of const in C++: when you start using const to declare that some things cannot be changed, then the compiler gets really finicky about every function properly declaring the const-ness of its parameters. It's valuable if you *completely* play by the rules; it's just a huge hassle if your commitment is anything less than 100 percent.

- Dynamically typed languages may let you play fast and loose with types, but it still doesn't make sense to call factorial() on a string. You need to use contract-oriented unit tests, discussed in Tip 3, *Design with Tests*, on page 21, to ensure that your functions adequately check the sanity of their parameters.

Regardless of the language's type system, get in the habit of documenting your expectations of each parameter—they usually aren't as self-explanatory as the factorial(n) example. See Tip 6, *Be Stylish*, on page 41 for further discussion of documentation and code comments.

The Misnomer of 100 Percent Coverage

A common (but flawed) metric for answering "Have I tested enough?" is code coverage. That is, what percentage of your application code is exercised by running the unit tests? Ideally, every line of code in your application gets run at least once while running the unit tests—coverage is 100 percent.

Less than 100 percent coverage means you have some cases that are not tested. Junior programmers will assume that the converse is true: when they hit 100 percent coverage, they have enough tests. However, that's not true: 100 percent coverage *absolutely does not* mean that all cases are covered.

Consider the following C code:

BadStringReverse.c
```c
#include <assert.h>
#include <stdio.h>
#include <stdlib.h>
#include <string.h>

void reverse(char *str) // BAD BAD BAD
{
        int len = strlen(str);
        char *copy = malloc(len);

        for (int i = 0; i < len; i++) {
                copy[i] = str[len - i - 1];
        }
        copy[len] = 0;

        strcpy(str, copy);
}

int main()
{
        char str[] = "fubar";
        reverse(str);
        assert(strcmp(str, "rabuf") == 0);
        printf("Ta-da, it works!\n"); // Not quite
}
```

The test covers 100 percent of the reverse function. Does that mean the function is correct? No: the memory allocated by malloc() is never freed, and the allocated buffer is one byte too small.

Don't be lulled into complacency by 100 percent coverage: *it means nothing about the quality of your code or your tests.*

Writing good tests, just like writing good application code, requires thought, diligence, and good judgment.

Less Than 100 Percent Coverage

Some cases can be extremely hard to unit test. Here's an example:

- Kernel drivers that interface with hardware rely on hardware state changes outside your code's control, and creating a high-fidelity test double is near impossible.

- Multithreaded code can have timing problems that require sheer luck to fall into.

- Third-party code provided as binaries often can't be provoked to return failures at will.

So, how do you get 100 percent coverage from your tests? With enough wizardry, it's surely possible, but is it worth it? That's a value judgment that may come down to *no*. In those situations, discuss the issue with your team's tech lead. They may be able to think of a test method that's not too painful. If nothing else, you will need them to review your code.

Don't be dissuaded if you can't hit 100 percent, and don't use that as an excuse to punt on testing entirely. Prove what's reasonable with tests; subject everything else to review by a senior programmer.

Further Reading

Kent Beck's *Test-Driven Development: By Example* [Bec02] remains a foundational work on unit testing. Although it uses Java in its examples, the principles apply to any language. (While reading it, try to solve the example problem in your own way; you may come up with a more elegant solution.) We'll discuss the test-driven aspect in Tip 3, *Design with Tests*, on page 21.

For complete coverage of the Ruby Way to unit testing, Ruby programmers should pick up *The RSpec Book* [CADH09].

C programmers should look to *Test Driven Development for Embedded C* [Gre10] for techniques on TDD and building test harnesses.

There's a nomenclature around test doubles; terms like *mocks* and *stubs* have specific definitions. Martin Fowler has a good article online[4] that explains the details.

There's a whole theory around type systems and using them to build correct code; see Pierce's *Types and Programming Languages* [Pie02] for the gory details. Also, Kim Bruce's *Foundations of Object-Oriented Languages: Types and Semantics* [Bru02] has specific emphasis on OOP.

Actions

- Look up the unit testing frameworks available for each programming language you use. Most languages will have both the usual bases covered (assertions, test setup, and teardown) and some facility for fake objects (mocks, stubs). Install any tools you need to get these running.

- This tip has bits and pieces of a program that reads lines of comma-separated data from a file, splits them apart, and uses them to create objects. Create a program that does this in the language of your choice, complete with unit tests that assure the correctness of every line of application code.

---

4. http://martinfowler.com/articles/mocksArentStubs.html

Tip 3

Design with Tests

 [*Brown Belt*]   You may not start designing new code right up front, but you will soon enough.

Where our previous tip, Tip 2, *Insist on Correctness*, on page 11, focused on making sure your code does what it's supposed to do, here we focus on the meta-question, "What should this code do?"

On the surface, it would seem puzzling that a programmer would write code without knowing, well ahead of time, what it's supposed to do. Yet we do it all the time. Faced with a problem, we charge off writing code and figure things out as we go. Programming is a creative act, not a mechanical one, and this process is akin to a painter charging off on a blank canvas without knowing *exactly* what the finished painting will look like. (Is this why so much code resembles a Jackson Pollock painting?)

Yet programming also requires rigor. Testing gives you tools for both design and rigor at the same time.

Designing with Tests

Thanks to frameworks for test doubles, discussed in *Interactions*, on page 13, you can start with a big programming problem and start attacking it from whatever angle makes sense first. Perhaps your program needs to grab an XML file with customer statistics, wade through it, and produce summary stats of the data. You're not sure offhand how to parse the XML, but you *do* know how to calculate the average customer age. No problem, mock the XML parsing and test the calculation:

AverageCustomerAge.rb

```ruby
class TestCustomerStats < Test::Unit::TestCase
  def test_mean_age
    data =
      [{:name => 'A', :age => 33},
       {:name => 'B', :age => 25}]
    CustomerStats.expects(:parse_xml).returns(data)
    File.expects(:read).returns(nil)

    stats = CustomerStats.load
    assert_equal 29, stats.mean_age
  end
end
```

Now you can write that code:

AverageCustomerAge.rb

```ruby
class CustomerStats
  def initialize
    @customers = []
  end

  def self.load
    xml = File.read('customer_database.xml')
    stats = CustomerStats.new
    stats.append parse_xml(xml)
    stats
  end

  def append(data)
    @customers += data
  end

  def mean_age
    sum = @customers.inject(0) { |s, c| s += c[:age] }
    sum / @customers.length
  end
end
```

Confident that you have that part nailed, you can move on to parsing XML. Take a couple of entries out of the huge customer database, just enough to make sure you have the format right:

data/customers.xml

```xml
<customers>

  <customer>
    <name>Alice</name>
    <age>33</age>
  </customer>
```

```
  <customer>
    <name>Bob</name>
    <age>25</age>
  </customer>
</customers>
```

Next, here's a simple test to validate the parsing:

AverageCustomerAge.rb
```
def test_parse_xml
  stats = CustomerStats.parse_xml(
    canned_data_from 'customers.xml')
  assert_equal 2, stats.length
  assert_equal 'Alice', stats.first[:name]
end
```

From there you can start picking apart the XML:

AverageCustomerAge.rb
```
def self.parse_xml(xml)
  entries = []
  doc = REXML::Document.new(xml)

  doc.elements.each('//customer') do |customer|
    entries.push({
      :name => customer.elements['name'].text,
      :age => customer.elements['age'].text.to_i })
  end

  entries
end
```

You have the flexibility to design from the top down, bottom up, or anywhere in between. You can start with either the part that's riskiest (that is, what you're most worried about) or the part you have the most confidence in.

Tests are serving several purposes here: first, they're allowing you to move quickly since you can do hand-wavy mocking for your code's interactions with outside components. "I know I'll need to get this data from XML, but let's assume some other method did that already." Second, the tests naturally drive a modular style of construction—it's simply *easier* to do it that way. Last, the tests stick around and ensure that you (or a future maintainer) don't break something on accident.

Tests As Specification

At some point you have a good idea of what each function should do. Now is the time to tighten down the screws: what *precisely* should the function do in the happy path? What shouldn't it do? How should it fail? Think of it as a specification: you tell the computer—and the programmer who needs to maintain your code five years from now—your exact expectations.

Let's start with an easy example, a factorial function. First question: what should it do? By definition, factorial *n* is the product of all positive integers less than or equal to *n*. Factorial of zero is a special case that's one. These rules are easy enough to express as Ruby unit tests:

Factorial.rb
```ruby
def test_valid_input
  assert_equal 1, 0.factorial
  assert_equal 1, 1.factorial
  assert_equal 2, 2.factorial
  assert_equal 6, 3.factorial
end
```

In choosing values to test, I'm testing the valid boundary condition (zero) and enough values to establish the factorial pattern. You could test a few more, for the sake of illustration, but it's not strictly necessary.

The next question to ask is, what's invalid input? Negative numbers come to mind. So do floats. (Technically there is such a thing as factorial for noninteger numbers and complex numbers,[5] but let's keep this simple.) Let's express those constraints as well:

Factorial.rb
```ruby
def test_raises_on_negative_input
  assert_raise(ArgumentError) { -1.factorial }
end

def test_factorial_does_not_work_on_floats
  assert_raise(NoMethodError) { 1.0.factorial }
end
```

I chose to raise an ArgumentError exception for negative integers and let Ruby raise a NoMethodError for calling factorial on objects of any other type.

---

5. http://en.wikipedia.org/wiki/Factorial

That's a reasonably complete specification. In fact, from there the code itself pretty much writes itself. (Go ahead, write a factorial function that passes the tests.)

Over-Testing

When programmers start unit testing, a common question arises: what are all the values I need to test? You could test hundreds of values for the factorial function, for example, but does that tell you anything more? No.

Therefore, *test what's needed to specify the behavior of the function.* That includes both the happy path and the error cases. *Then stop.*

Aside from wasting time, do additional tests do any harm? Yes:

- Unit tests are valuable as a specification, so additional clutter makes it hard for the reader to discern the important parts of the specification from needless fluff.

- Every line of code is potentially buggy—even test code. Debugging test code that doesn't need to be there is a *double* waste of time.

- If you decide to change the interface to your module, you have more tests to change as well.

Therefore, write only the tests you need to verify correctness.

Further Reading

Growing Object-Oriented Software, Guided by Tests [FP09] has extensive coverage of the design process with TDD and mocking.

As before, Ruby programmers will benefit tremendously from *The RSpec Book* [CADH09].

If it occurred to you that "tests as specifications" sounds an awful lot like inductive proofs, you're right. You can read a lot more about inductive proofs in *The Algorithm Design Manual* [Ski97].

Industry Perspective: A Different Opinion

A lot of people spend a lot of time up front designing and figuring out how to break up a problem into pieces—nowadays, how to break it up into classes—and I argue that whatever decisions you make up front will be wrong.

My advice contradicts popular wisdom: start coding as soon as possible. When you're looking at a problem, *do it wrong first.*

When I'm programming, I make a prototype with just a few big classes. Then I write the production code once I have a better picture of the problem. Too often now, programmers break things up into classes up front, and then they force their implementation onto a structure that they created when they didn't have enough information.

–Scott "Zz" Zimmerman, senior software engineer

Actions

In the beginning of this tip, we used some data encoded in XML. This is a very common task in industry, so it's useful to practice with loading and saving XML.

Start with a very simple structure, like the previous customer list snippet. Use a prebuilt parser, like REXML for Ruby, for the actual parsing, because you'll want to stick to the issues of what to do with the parser's results. Before you run off and write any code, think of tests you'd construct for a function that loads that XML:

- What happens when there are no customers in the list?

- How should you handle a field that's blank?

- What about invalid characters, like letters in the age field?

With those questions answered and expressed as tests, now write the loader function.

Bonus round: build some tests for manipulating the customer list and saving it back to a file. You can use an XML generator like Builder for Ruby.

Tip 4

Tame Complexity

 [*White Belt*] You'll be dealing with complex code from day one.

If you've never met a program you couldn't understand, you haven't been programming long enough. In industry, it won't be long before you run into a mind-bogglingly gnarly mess of code: The Behemoth, The Spaghetti Factory, The Legacy System from Hell. I once inherited a program whose previous owner, upon hearing that he'd have to add a substantial new feature, quit his job instead. (And I couldn't blame him.)

Complexity in software systems is unavoidable; some problems are just hard, and their solutions are complex. However, much of the complexity you find in software is a mess of our own making. In his book *The Mythical Man-Month* [Bro95], Fred Brooks separates the two sources of complexity into *necessary* and *accidental* complexity.

Here's a way to think about the difference between necessary and accidental complexity: what complexity is inherent in the *problem domain*? Say you're faced with a program that has date/time-handling code scattered all over the place. There's some necessary complexity when handling time: months have different numbers of days, you have to consider leap years, and so forth. But most programs I've seen have loads of accidental complexity relating to time: times stored in different formats, novel (and buggy) methods to add and subtract times, inconsistent formats for printing times, and much more.

The Complexity Death Spiral

It's very common in programming that the accidental complexity in a product's code base gradually overwhelms the

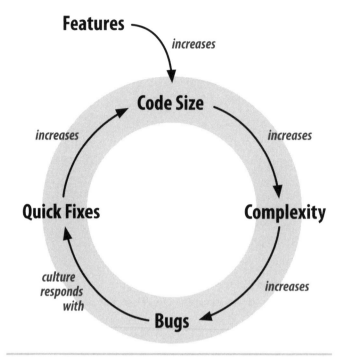

Figure 1—The complexity death spiral

necessary complexity. At some point, things devolve into a self-amplifying phenomenon that I call the *complexity death spiral*, illustrated in Figure 1, *The complexity death spiral*, on page 28.

Problem 1: Code Size

As you build a product, its code size will grow vastly beyond any school or hobby project. Code bases in industry are measured in *thousands* to *millions* of lines of code (LOC).

In *Lions' Commentary on UNIX 6th Edition* [Lio77], John Lions commented that 10,000 lines of code is the practical limit of program size that a single programmer can understand and maintain. *UNIX 6th Edition*, released back in 1975, weighed in at 9,000 LOC (minus machine-specific device drivers).

By comparison, in 1993 Windows NT had 4 to 5 million lines of code. Ten years later, Windows Server 2003 had 2,000 developers and 2,000 testers who managed a whopping 50 million LOC.[6] Most industry projects aren't as big as Windows, but they're well past the 10,000 mark that Lions drew in the sand. This scale means that *there is nobody in the company who understands the whole code base.*

Problem 2: Complexity

As products grow in size, the conceptual elegance of the original idea gets lost. What was once a crystal-clear idea to the two guys in their garage becomes a murky swamp with dozens of developers wading through it.

Complexity does not *necessarily* follow code size; it is possible for a large code base to be broken into many modules, each with a clear purpose, elegant implementation, and well-known interactions with neighboring modules.

However, even well-designed systems become complex when they become large. When no single person can understand the whole system, then by necessity multiple people must each keep *their* idea of *their* piece of the system in their head—and nobody has exactly the same idea.

Problem 3: Bugs

As the product soars in complexity, bugs inevitably come along for the ride. No way around it—even great programmers aren't perfect. But not all bugs are created equal: the ones in a highly complex system are especially nasty to track down. Ever hear a programmer say, "I dunno, man, the system just crashed." Welcome to debugging in hell.

Problem 4: Quick Fixes

The question isn't whether the product will have bugs or not—it will. The question is how the engineering team responds. Under pressure to get the product out the door, all too often programmers resort to quick fixes.

The quick fix patches over the problem rather than addresses the root cause. Often the root cause isn't even found. Here's an example:

---

6. http://en.wikipedia.org/wiki/Source_lines_of_code

LOC Is a Measure of Weight, Not Progress

Managers strive to measure things, and since building a software product means writing code, it makes sense—on the surface—to measure a product's progress by its lines of code. However, this is a fundamentally misguided measure since *good* programmers seek elegant solutions, and elegance tends to use fewer LOC than brute-force solutions.

LOC is a useful measure of *something*, but it's not progress: it's a measure of weight. Bill Gates observed that measuring programming progress by lines of code is like measuring aircraft building progress by weight.[a]

You don't need to be an aerospace engineer to understand that you should build an aircraft as light as possible—any extra weight makes the plane less efficient. However, planes are still heavy. An Airbus A380 weighs a whopping 610,000 pounds. It also carries about 650 people. (A Cessna 172, by comparison, weighs a measly 1,620 pounds and carries four—but not gracefully, and there's no beverage cart.)

Likewise, a feature-rich product is going to have a lot of code in it; there's no getting around that. But the product should be as lean as it can get away with, because every extra LOC will just weigh down its future development.

---

a.   http://c2.com/cgi/wiki?LinesOfCode

PROGRAMMER: *The program crashes when it tries to put a job on the network queue but the queue doesn't respond within ten seconds.*

MANAGER: *Make it retry the queue operation a hundred times.*

What's the root cause? Who knows, with enough retries you can patch over just about anything. But as with auto body repair, at some point there's more Bondo than actual car left.

The more insidious problem is that when a fix doesn't address the root cause of a problem, the problem usually doesn't go away at all—it just moves somewhere else. In the previous dialogue, perhaps retrying a hundred times covers up the problem pretty well, but what happens when 101 retries are needed? The manager just pulled the number out of thin air, and the Bondo fix just made the problem harder to see.

Pile on the quick fixes, and now we've come full-circle to increased code size.

Toward Clarity

When people think of the opposite of complex, they usually think *simple*. However, because of the necessary complexity of our field, we can't always write simple code. The better opposite of complex is *clear*. Is it clear to the reader what your code is doing?

Two facets to clarity help us reduce accidental software complexity: clarity of *thought* and clarity of *expression*.

Clear Thought

When we reason about a problem, we seek to make a clear statement like "There should be exactly one way to store a time." Why, then, does Unix C code have a mix of time structures like time_t, struct timeval, and struct timespec?[8] That's not so clear.

How do you reconcile your clear statement with the complexity of Unix timekeeping? You need to fence off the complexity, or *abstract* it into a single module. In C this might be a structure and functions that operate on it; in C++ it would be a class. Modular design allows the rest of your program to reason about time in a clear manner without knowing the innards of the system's timekeeping.

Once you can reason about time as a separate module of your program, you can also *prove* that your timekeeping is correct. The best way to do this is with separate tests, but a peer review or written specification would also work. It's far easier to test and rigorously prove a chunk of logic when it's separate than when it's embedded in a larger body of code.

Clear Expression

As you think clearly about a module and isolate it from the rest of your program, the resulting program also expresses its purpose more clearly, too. Your code dealing with the problem domain should truly focus on the problem domain.

---

8.   http://en.wikipedia.org/wiki/Unix_time

As you pull secondary code out into its own modules, the remaining logic should read more and more like a specification of the problem domain (though perhaps with more semicolons).

Let's look at a before-and-after comparison. I've seen this kind of C++ code numerous times:

```
Time.cpp
void do_stuff_with_progress1()
{
    struct timeval start;
    struct timeval now;

    gettimeofday(&start, 0);
    // Do stuff, printing a progress message
    // every half second
    while (true) {
        struct timeval elapsed;
        gettimeofday(&now, 0);
        timersub(&now, &start, &elapsed);

        struct timeval interval;
        interval.tv_sec = 0;
        interval.tv_usec = 500 * 1000; // 500ms

        if (timercmp(&elapsed, &interval, >)) {
            printf("still working on it...\n");
            start = now;
        }
        // Do stuff...
    }
}
```

The point of the loop is the "do stuff" part, but there's twenty lines of POSIX timekeeping gunk before you ever get there. There's nothing incorrect about it, but...*ugh*. Isn't there a way to keep the loop focused on its problem domain rather than timekeeping?

Let's pull all the time gunk into its own class:

```
Time.cpp
class Timer
{
public:
    Timer(const time_t sec, const suseconds_t usec) {
        _interval.tv_sec = sec;
        _interval.tv_usec = usec;
        gettimeofday(&_start, 0);
    }
```

```
    bool triggered() {
        struct timeval now;
        struct timeval elapsed;

        gettimeofday(&now, 0);
        timersub(&now, &_start, &elapsed);

        return timercmp(&elapsed, &_interval, >);
    }

    void reset() {
        gettimeofday(&_start, 0);
    }

private:
    struct timeval _interval;
    struct timeval _start;
};
```

Now we can simplify the loop:

Time.cpp
```
void do_stuff_with_progress2()
{
    Timer progress_timer(0, 500 * 1000); // 500ms

    // Do stuff, printing a progress message
    // every half second
    while (true) {
        if (progress_timer.triggered()) {
            printf("still working on it...\n");
            progress_timer.reset();
        }

        // Do stuff...
    }
}
```

The computer is doing the same stuff in both cases, but consider what the second example does for the program's maintainability:

- The Timer class can be tested and proven independent of its use in the program.

- The timekeeping in the "do stuff" loop has meaningful semantics—triggered() and reset()—rather than a bunch of get, add, and compare functions.

- It's now clear where the timekeeping ends and the (fictional) meat of the loop begins.

As you work on code that's big and gnarly, consider this for each part: what is this code trying to say? Is there a way to say it more clearly? If it's a problem of clear expression, you may need to abstract out the bits that are getting in the way, as with the Timer class shown earlier. If the code is still a mess, it may be the product of unclear thought, and that needs rework at the design level.

Actions

Focus on one aspect of programming—like timekeeping—that can be isolated and reasoned about rigorously. Dig through the project you're working on and identify places where the code could be made clearer if that logic was abstracted into its own module.

Try your hand at a more modular approach: take a couple places where things are messy and separate the necessary complexity from the accidental complexity. Don't sweat the details at this point; just see how clearly you can express the necessary business logic, with the assumption that you have separate modules to handle the supporting logic.

Fail Gracefully

 [*White Belt*]   Writing code that fails well is just as important as writing code that works well.

What happens when code fails? It's going to. Even if you wrote *your* part perfectly, there are all kinds of conditions that could cause the overall system to fail:

- A rogue mail daemon on computer, busy sending offers of great wealth from some foreign country, consumes all the RAM and swap. Your next call to malloc() returns ETOOMUCHSPAM.

- Java Update 134,001 fills up the system's hard drive. You call write(), and the system returns ESWITCHTODECAF.

- You try to pull data off a tape, but the tape robot is on a ship at sea, rolling waves cause the robot to drop the tape, and the driver returns EROBOTDIZZY.

- Cosmic rays flip a bit in memory, causing a memory access to return 0x10000001 instead of 0x1, and you discover that this makes for a very bad parameter to pass into memcpy() after it returns EMEMTRASHED.

You may think, "Yeah, right" but all these cases actually happened. (Yes, I had to fix a tape robot controller because it would drop tapes when on a Navy ship.) Your code cannot naively assume that the world around it is sane—the world will take every opportunity to prove it wrong.

How your code fails is just as important as how it works. You may not be able to *fix* the failure, but if nothing else, your code should strive to fail gracefully.

Order of Operations

In many textbook programs, their environment is a clean slate, and the program runs to completion. In many messy, nontextbook programs, the environment is a rugby match of threads and resources, all seemingly trying to beat each other into submission.

Consider the following example: you're creating a list of customer names and addresses that will be fed to a label printer. Your code gets passed a customer ID and a database connection, so you need to query the database for what you need. You create a linked list whose add() method looks like this:

```
ListUpdate.rb
def add(customer_id) # BAD BAD BAD, see text
  begin
    @mutex.lock
    old_head = @head
    @head = Customer.new
    @head.name =
      @database.query(customer_id, :name)
    @head.address =
      @database.query(customer_id, :address)
    @head.next = old_head
  ensure
    @mutex.unlock
  end
end
```

(Yes, I know this example is contrived. Bear with me.)

This code works in the happy path: the new element is put at the head of the list, it gets filled in, and everything is happy. But what if one of those queries to the database raises an exception? Take a look at the code again.[9]

This code doesn't fail gracefully. In fact, it does collateral damage by allowing a database failure to destroy the customer list. The culprit is the order of operations:

- The list @head and @head.next are absolutely vital to the list's integrity. These shouldn't be monkeyed with until everything else is ready.

---

9. Answer: First, the head of the list has already been set to the new element, so the head will have at least one blank field. Second, the rest of the list will vanish because head.next gets updated only after the database queries. And bonus badness: the list stays locked for the duration of the database queries—operations that could take an indeterminate amount of time to complete.

- The new object should be fully constructed before inserting into the list.

- The lock should not be held during operations that could block. (Assume there's other threads wanting to read the list.)

Transactions

In the previous section, the example had only one essential bit of state that needed to stay consistent. What about cases where there's more than one? Consider the classic example of moving money between two bank accounts:

```
Transaction.rb
savings.deduct(100)
checking.deposit(100)
```

What happens if the database croaks right after the money has been deducted and the deposit into checking fails? Where did the money go? Perhaps you try to solve that case by putting it back into the savings account:

```
Transaction.rb
savings.deduct(100)       # Happily works
begin
  checking.deposit(100)   # Fails: database went down!
rescue
  begin
    # Put money back
    savings.deposit(100) # Fails: database still dead
  rescue
    # Now what???
  end
end
```

Nice try, but that doesn't help if the second deposit() fails, too.

The tool you need here is a *transaction*. Its purpose is to allow several operations, potentially to several objects, to be either fulfilled completely or rolled back.

Transactions (here in a made-up system) would allow our previous example to look like this:

```
Transaction.rb
t = Transaction.new(savings, checking)
t.start
```

```
# Inject failure
checking.expects(:deposit).with(100).raises

begin
  savings.deduct(100)
  checking.deposit(100)
  t.commit
rescue
  t.rollback
end
```

You'll usually find transactions in databases, because our example scenario is exceedingly common in that field. You may find variations on this theme anywhere systems require an all-or-nothing interlock.

Failure Injection

So far, we've talked about how your code responds to *likely* failures. For purposes of testing, how do you ensure your code responds well when an essential resource dies, passes on, is no more, ceases to be, pushes up daisies, and becomes an ex-resource?

The solution is to inject failures using an automated test harness. This is easiest with a mock object framework, because you can tell the mock to return good data several times and then return something bogus or throw an exception. Likewise, in the code under test, you assert that the appropriate exception is raised.

Revisiting our list update problem, here's some test code that simulates a valid database response for key 1 and a failure on the query for key 2:

ListUpdate2.rb
```
require 'rubygems'
require 'test/unit'
require 'mocha'

class ListUpdateTest < Test::Unit::TestCase
  def test_database_failure
    database = mock()
    database.expects(:query).with(1, :name).
      returns('Anand')
    database.expects(:query).with(1, :address).
      returns('')
    database.expects(:query).with(2, :name).
      raises
```

```
    q = ShippingQueue.new(database)
    q.add(1)

    assert_raise(RuntimeError) do
②      q.add(2)
    end

    # List is still okay
③    assert_equal 'Anand', q.head.name
    assert_equal nil, q.head.next
  end
end
```

① Injection of RuntimeError exception.

② Call will raise; the assert_raise is expecting it (and will trap the exception).

③ Verify that the list is still intact, as if q.add(2) were never called.

Failure injection of this sort allows you to think through—and verify—each potential scenario of doom. Test in this manner just as often as you test the happy path.

Test Monkeys

You can think through scenarios all day long and build tremendously robust code. Yet most fool-proof programs can be foiled by a sufficiently talented fool. If you don't have such a fool handy, the next best thing is a *test monkey*.

In my first job working on handheld computers, we had a program called Monkey that would inject random taps and drags into the UI layer, as if they had come from the touch-screen. There was nothing fancier than that. We'd run Monkey until the system crashed.

Monkey may not have been a talented fool, but a whole bunch of monkeys tapping like mad, 24 hours a day, makes up for lack of talent. Alas, no Shakespeare (but perhaps some E. E. Cummings) and a whole bunch of crashes. The crashes were things we couldn't have envisioned—that was the point.

In the same way, can you create a test harness that beats the snot out of your program with random (but valid) data? Let it run thousands or millions of cycles; you never know what might turn up. I used this technique on a recent project and discovered that once in a blue moon, a vendor API function would return "unknown" for the state of a virtual machine. What do they mean, they *don't know* the state? I had no idea the function could return that. My program crashed when it happened. Lesson learned…again.

Actions

Revisit the previous code with the customer list. How would you fix it? Here's a shell to work with:

ListUpdate2.rb
```ruby
require 'thread'

class Customer
  attr_accessor :name, :address, :next

  def initialize
    @name = nil
    @address = nil
    @next = nil
  end
end

class ShippingQueue
  attr_reader :head

  def initialize(database)
    @database = database
    @head = nil
    @mutex = Mutex.new
  end

  def add(customer_id)
    # Fill in this part
  end
end
```

Use the test code from *Failure Injection*, on page 38 to see whether you got it right.

Tip 6

Be Stylish

 [*White Belt*]   Writing code with good style helps well before the professional world.

These two functions do exactly the same thing:

Fibonacci.c
```c
uint64_t
fibonacci(unsigned int n)
{
    if (n == 0 || n == 1) {
        return n;
    }
    else {
        uint64_t previous = 0;
        uint64_t current = 1;

        while (--n > 0) {
            uint64_t sum = previous + current;
            previous = current;
            current = sum;
        }

        return current;
    }
}
```

Fibonacci.c
```c
unsigned long long fbncci(unsigned int quux) { if
(quux == 0 || quux == 1) { return quux; } else {
unsigned long long foo = 0; unsigned long long bar
= 1; while (--quux > 0) { unsigned long long baz =
foo + bar; foo = bar; bar = baz; } return bar; } }
```

Which would you rather maintain?

Maybe that example is a little extreme, but it illustrates a simple point: your code isn't just read by a compiler; it's read by other programmers, too. Writing code with *good style* is a factor in software quality because you simply can't maintain code that you can't read.

Factors to Style

The broad term *style* refers to all the things that the compiler doesn't care about but humans do. Here are some examples:

- Naming of classes, methods, variables, files, and so on
- Arrangement of functions within a file and across files
- Comments
- Braces and parentheses (where optional)
- Choice of control structures (where equivalent)
- Capitalization
- Indentation and other whitespace

The definition of good style varies depending on the programmers you're working with, project or corporate style guides, and conventions established by the programming language. However, there are some common themes we'll look at here.

Why Naming Matters

Well-written code won't read like a human language, but it shouldn't read like alien hieroglyphics, either. Good naming of classes, methods, parameters, and variables will go a long way toward making the code read naturally to another programmer. This doesn't mean names need to be overly wordy; they just need to be appropriate to the problem domain.

Consider the Fibonacci code opening this tip. The variables previous, current, and sum are descriptive to their purpose. The parameter n is short but appropriate to the problem domain; the purpose of the function is to return the *n*th Fibonacci number. Similarly, i and j are often used as index variables in loops.

If you're struggling to name something, that's a tip-off that the purpose of your code may be questionable. Here is an example:

```
im = InfoManager.new
puts im.get_customer_name_and_zip_code(customer_id)
```

What exactly is an InfoManager? What do you do with one? How do you reason about one? Vague names like InfoManager usually indicate vague purpose. The method name should similarly tip you off to questionable code. Contrast that code with the following:

```
customer = Customer.find(customer_id)
puts customer.name
puts customer.address.zip_code
```

Objects like customers and addresses are things you can reason about, and natural-sounding method names—find(), name(), and so forth—should come, well, naturally.

Commentary

Legend speaks of the ultimate code comment of woe. It is, of course:

```
i = i + 1; /* add one to i */
```

Comments shouldn't tell the reader *how* the code works. The code should tell them that. If the code is not clear, fix the code to make it clear. Instead, focus comments on the following:

- What is the purpose of this code, if it's not intuitive? For example, the IMAP protocol defines the user's inbox as the special string INBOX, so a comment in your code could refer the reader to the appropriate section in the specification: list("INBOX"); /* mailbox INBOX is special, see RFC3501 section 5.1 */.

- What parameters and return values are expected? Some of this may be inferred from the names of the parameters, but for public APIs, a summary comment before the function can be useful. Also, many documentation generators can scan source files and generate summary docs for public APIs. JavaDoc[10] and Doxygen[11] are common tools for this task.

- Is there something you need to remember temporarily? Programmers will use strings such as TODO and FIXME to make a reminder to themselves during development.

---

10. http://java.sun.com/j2se/javadoc/
11. http://www.stack.nl/~dimitri/doxygen/

However, fix these strings before checking in: if you really need to do something later, put it in whatever system your team uses for tracking tasks. If it's a bug, fix it or enter a bug report. Source code is not your to-do list or bug database.

• What is the copyright and license for the file? It's normal practice to put a header comment in each file specifying the copyright ownership (typically your company) and any license terms. If in doubt, there is no license; it's "all rights reserved." Code contributed to open source projects needs to explicitly state a license.

Used properly, comments complement the code in a natural manner, giving future readers a clear picture of what's going on and why.

Conventions for Exits and Exceptions

This is part style, part correctness. Some style guides, typically for C code, specify that a function can have only one exit point. Often the origin for this rule is to ensure that any allocated resources are released. I've seen code similar to the following in several operating system kernels:

```c
ExitPoints.c
int
function()
{
    int err = 0;
    char *str = malloc(sizeof(char) * 5);

    if (str == NULL) {
        err = ENOMEM;
        goto ERROR;
    }

    // ...

    FILE *file = fopen("/tmp/foo", "w");

    if (file == NULL) {
        err = EIO;
        goto ERROR_FREE_STR;
    }

    // ...

    err = write_stuff(file);
```

```
    if (err != 0) {
        err = EIO;
        goto ERROR_CLOSE_FILE;
    }

    // ...

ERROR_CLOSE_FILE:
    fclose(file);
ERROR_FREE_STR:
    free(str);
ERROR:
    return err;
}
```

In the happy path, execution falls through the fclose() and free() at the bottom, releasing resources in the opposite order of their creation. The use of labels at the end allows error cases to simply set the desired return value and jump to where the correct resources are released. This is conceptually similar to throwing an exception, except that you call the "destructors" yourself. This technique can be less error prone than checking every return statement by hand.

Of course, other C style guides insist that you never, ever, on penalty of death, use a goto statement. If the company style guide insists on *both* a single exit point and no goto, prepare for some painful acrobatics to fulfill both rules.

Exceptions can use a similar strategy if you are calling APIs (like a C library) that don't provide a class with a constructor and destructor. However, it's often better to make a lightweight class that wraps the appropriate resource. Here's an example in C++:

OpenFile.cpp
```cpp
class open_file
{
  public:
    open_file(const char *name, const char *mode) {
        _file = fopen(name, mode);

        // ...raise exception here if NULL...
    }

    ~open_file() {
        fclose(_file);
    }
```

```
    // Conversion operator so instances can
    // be used as parameters to fprintf, etc.
    operator FILE*() {
        return _file;
    }

  private:
    FILE* _file;
};
```

In this example, an open_file instance can be created on the stack, and the file will be closed on return from a function, no matter if you leave with a return or an exception—C++ will call the destructors of any instances on the stack.

If in Doubt...

If your company has no coding style guide, fall back to the following:

- Match the style of any code you're editing. Even more annoying than poor style is a file with a mishmash of multiple styles.

- Follow any established language conventions. Some languages, like Ruby, have very well-established precedent for naming and indentation. When writing in Ruby, do like the Rubyists do.

- For languages with inconsistent precedent, like C++, follow the precedent of major libraries you're using. The C++ Standard Template Library has a consistent naming style, so it makes sense to match their style when using STL.

For projects with multiple languages, it still makes sense to follow conventions for each language—make Ruby look like Ruby, and make C++ look like C++. This goes beyond issues like naming and indentation; follow the idiom of each language as well. See *Idiomatic Programming*, on page 71 for further discussion. Provide a bridge layer if needed.

Further Reading

Take a look at Robert C. Martin's *Clean Code* [Mar08]; it's an authoritative work on coding style.

Consult Wikipedia[12] for links to a large assortment of style guides.

Actions

Find a style guide (sometimes under the name *coding standards*) for a language you use, preferably one that explains the rationale for each of its rules. Some rules will be arbitrary, but most have the intention of reducing accidental bugs or improving readability. Read it for the *why* behind the rules more than the *what*.

---

12. http://en.wikipedia.org/wiki/Programming_style

Tip 7

Improve Legacy Code

 [*White Belt*]   Maintaining and improving legacy code is a day-one reality.

Your job would (seemingly) be a lot easier if you could simply take all the crappy old code floating around, trash it, and start over. But that's not going to happen, so what do you do about it?

The typical Godzilla legacy code base looks something like this:

- Functions spanning thousands of lines, with a near-infinite number of possible code paths.

- Classes or modules with dependencies on twenty (or more) other classes.

- A comment somewhere reads, "Don't touch this or everything will break!"

- Another comment reads, "Ask Bob before changing this code," where Bob is a programmer who left the company a decade ago.

- …and much, much more.

Sometimes when you need to fix a bug in code like this, the path of least resistance—just making the change without cleaning anything up—is the most prudent path. However, consider the maxim "If you find yourself in a hole, stop digging." If this is code you'll need to maintain for some time, it's best to make things better as you go.

Finding Seams

The key problem with legacy cleanup is where to start. If everything depends on everything else, how can you separate a module to work on? Let's say you're working on a

> ## Industry Perspective: Making Inroads in Legacy Code
>
> When getting started in a legacy project, pick some very minor thing, make a very minor change, and observe the impact. It would be nice if this legacy code base had a comprehensive suite of tests, but it won't. Worse, it may have been designed in such a way that testing it is virtually impossible.
>
> Adding test cases is likely to be difficult. The code will be tangled and tightly coupled, and teasing apart even a little bit of it to put into test will only put the parts into test that are relatively trivial anyway. The truly hard stuff will be very resistant to being made testable.
>
> This is the hardest part of the battle. You have to find a place to plant your flag of progress and write a test that sanely and clearly controls the behavior of that part of the system and defend it valiantly. Once you have made one inroad, find a direction to grow that and doggedly pursue it.
>
> —*Rich Rector, engineering manager, Spectra Logic*

legacy Win32 application and you're porting it to POSIX. The system APIs are a good place to start. Perhaps start with file I/O, looking for stuff like the following:

```
HANDLE hFile;

if (CreateFile(hFile, GENERIC_READ, 0, 0,
               OPEN_EXISTING, 0, 0)) ==
               INVALID_HANDLE_VALUE) {
    // ...error handling...
}
```

Rather than replacing 100 calls to the Win32 API with 100 POSIX calls, take the opportunity to extract file I/O to its own module. (Or, use an existing cross-platform library like Apache Portable Runtime.[13]) Implement this module for both Win32 and POSIX, because this will allow you to verify the program's behavior on both platforms.

The practice of extracting bits of functionality is sometimes called *finding the seams* since you're looking for natural places you can pull the legacy code apart. Although there may not be many seams at first, it gets better as you go. Each newly

---

13. http://apr.apache.org/

built module is modular and well-tested, thereby giving you a bigger safety net when it's time to pull at the next level of seams.

Transition to New Platforms and Languages

The computing world never stays still, and legacy systems sometimes need to migrate just to stay functional. Perhaps it's just porting from some ancient versions of Windows to the current version; in a more ambitious project, it could be moving a system from PCs to the Web.

Where possible, contain migration risk by reusing parts of the old program. Here's an example:

- If the old program is written in a common language like C, many other programming languages have an option for interfacing with C code (Java Native Interface, Ruby extensions, and so on).

- If the old program has a network or console interface, you could build a shim layer that interacts with that by screen-scraping. You may laugh, but this is very common for building new front ends to ancient mainframe systems.

These may not be the best solutions for creating a maintainable system, but they could possibly buy you time. Consider an alternative scenario: the company's legacy system is on a version of Windows with a thousand known security flaws, everyone is panicked about getting the system migrated *now*, and they're willing to cut every corner possible. Taking an intermediate step—and buying your team the time to do the job right—suddenly doesn't sound so bad.

Bugs vs. Misfeatures

A common task for newbie programmers is bug patrol. Lucky you. When fixing bugs in legacy code, be careful to mentally separate bugs (clearly wrong behavior) from things that are simply strange. Fixing strangeness can bite you in ways you may not anticipate.

Let's say you're working on a web browser, and it crashes if it tries to generate a certain HTTP header field. That sounds like an obvious bug to fix. However, while fixing that bug, you also notice that the browser creates an HTTP header labeled "Referer," which is misspelled. Do you fix it?

In this case, no. Lots of web servers depend on that misspelling—in fact, it dates back to RFC 1945, from the mid-90s. "Fixing" that header would break all kinds of stuff.

That's not to say you shouldn't try to fix strangeness. Just be conscious that the code *might* be strange for a reason. Ask your mentor or a senior programmer. At a minimum, document your change in the check-in comments so others can find it quickly, just in case that bug was a misfeature in disguise.

Further Reading

Most programming books focus on writing new code. You can't blame the authors or the programmers buying the books; green-field programming is certainly a lot more fun. However, there are a couple books dedicated to "brownfield" programming.

Michael Feathers' *Working Effectively with Legacy Code* [Fea04] is the definitive text on dealing with legacy code. If you're working on a big legacy project, this is the book for you.

On a more tactical level, Martin Fowler's *Refactoring: Improving the Design of Existing Code* [FBBO99] is helpful for anyone maintaining code over time.

Actions

Some open source projects have a long history, yet they haven't devolved into the spaghetti mess of traditional legacy code. Consider the Apache HTTP Server,[14] initially released in 1995, or FreeBSD,[15] initially released in 1993. As of this writing, both are actively developed.

A hallmark of both projects is their clean code base. Assuming some knowledge of C, you can pick files at random and readily understand what the code is doing. So, along those lines:

---

14. http://projects.apache.org/projects/http_server.html
15. http://www.freebsd.org/

- Download source code for one of these projects, or view code using their online source browser.

- Observe their adherence to a single coding style and how that makes it easy to skim through pages of source code.

- Note how they've abstracted common patterns into separate libraries, for example the Apache Portable Runtime,[16] which makes the core code much easier to follow.

- Consider: these projects may be *old,* yet unlike *legacy* projects, there's little drive to replace them with something newer. How have they managed to keep up with the times?

- Consider: do these projects use programming techniques or standards that you could adopt in your company?

---

16. http://apr.apache.org/

Tip 8

Review Code Early and Often

 [*Brown Belt*]   Your code may not be peer reviewed on day one, but expect it within the first several months.

Many programmers loathe, detest, and double-plus unlike code reviews, but there's really no reason to hate them. In fact, experienced programmers *look forward* to code reviews —we'll see why shortly.

Person and Perspective

The reason so many code reviews go bad is because the programmer makes a connection between their *code's* worth and their *self*-worth. When reviewers point out problems in the code, the programmer takes it as an insult and gets defensive, and things go downhill quickly.

Let's be very clear about this: reviewers will find fault in your code. Gonna happen. I guarantee it. *That does not mean you suck.* There's always room for improvement, or at least different perspectives, on how your code should be written. Treat the code review as an open discussion, not a trial where you're the defendant.

"Faults" can range from bugs to issues of style. The bugs are easy; you have to fix them. Everyone, novice and expert alike, screws up now and then, so nobody in the room thinks you're an idiot. Just take a note and move on.

The more contentious problems arise with issues of style. Maybe you're using a loop with a counter and a senior programmer reviewing your work suggests using an iterator instead. Is your code *wrong* and the suggestion *right?* No, matters of style are not so absolute.

Since this is an open discussion, go ahead and discuss the merits of the suggestion. Perhaps the reviewer will say, "Using an iterator eliminates the possibility of an off-by-one problem." Don't get defensive and argue "But my loop doesn't have an off-by-one problem!" The reviewer knows that already. The point he's trying to make is, it's *good style* to eliminate that possibility with a different approach.

Once you understand the point the reviewer is making, thank him for the suggestion, take a note, and move on. Consider your course of action after you've had time to let the tension of the code review dissipate. Disagreements on style become contentious because they become personal; if you consider the merits of the disagreement without the other person right there, you may discover the reviewer had a valid point.

Perspective is essential: it's not about you being right and the reviewer being wrong. It's about good code and better code.

Formats

I'll describe the formats I've seen for code reviews and give you some tips for each.

The Ad Hoc Review

Often you're puzzled by something, and you just need someone to help you through it. Or perhaps you've found what you *think* is a good solution, but you're not sure. Go grab a more experienced programmer. Even the grumpy ones usually put their grumpiness on hold; the flattery of being asked for their opinion softens even the most surly.

Buddy System

Some projects will require a "buddy" to sign off on any code that's checked into the source repository. You've made a change, tested it, and now you need someone to review it before check-in. Do *not* just go find your favorite pal who will green-light anything you write. Go find someone who is an expert in the area you're changing. Failing that, find someone who hasn't buddied for you in a while.

Use the buddy system as a way to get more people familiar with your work. Especially when you're the new person, there's no better way to build your credibility than with code. It doesn't have to be brilliant, wicked, fancy code—just solid code. Make sure people see it on a regular basis.

The High-Level Review

This is often a sit-down meeting with multiple people and a projector. You're often reviewing weeks of work but at a high level. You explain the design, explain how it translates to code, and then review key portions of code. This is an opportunity for discussions on design and style. Be prepared for criticism, and keep in mind the issues I discussed about people and perspective.

My favorite question, as a reviewer, is "Let me see the tests." I require automated tests for any project I lead, so if the response to this question is a blank stare, the review is over, and we'll schedule a new one for the next week. However, the experienced programmer will *start* the review by going over the tests. Nothing instills confidence in your code better than showing the tests.

The Line-by-Line Review

The most tedious, soul-crushing code review is where everyone walks through the code line by line. In practice, this kind of review tends to be held for code that's already a disaster. (Better not be *your* code.) Given that you're in bug-hunting mode, ask of each line of code: what are the assumptions of this line? What ways could it fail? What happens in the failure case?

How do you avoid the line-by-line review of your code? Easy: get your code reviewed early and often. Use ad hoc or the buddy system, or schedule your own group reviews. I started by saying that experienced programmers *look forward* to code reviews. That's because they prefer to get feedback early and avoid getting into the mess that requires the line-by-line review.

The Audit

I've heard about this practice from others but not used it myself. In an audit, a senior programmer takes your entire project and drills down on specific topics. And when I say drill down, I mean way down. Why did you choose such-and-such design? What data did you have to prove your assumptions? How do you prove (or test) that your implementation is correct? How much wood could it chuck per second if it could chuck wood? You get the idea.

Preparing for an audit is a big deal because you don't know what the auditor is going to ask. You have to be prepared for anything. My only advice here is to ask yourself the same kinds of questions as you program. If your program is reading data from a file, ask yourself, what assumptions am I making of that file's format? How am I testing those assumptions? How big can the file be? Can I prove that?

Of course, you can follow the rabbit hole down only so far. At some point there's a diminishing return on this line of thinking; that point will vary depending on the type of project and the phase of its life cycle. Err on the side of caution with production code. Err on the side of git-er-done with trade show demos or proofs of concept.

Code Review Policies

Policies surrounding code reviews range from nonexistent to institutional. If the development style of the team is on the chaotic end of the spectrum, they probably don't do code reviews unless absolutely necessary. That's when you have the line-by-line review that saps your will to live. If the team uses a development practice like Extreme Programming, code review is constant: XP's pair programming, in effect, reviews the code as it's written.

Some industries require code review for certification purposes. If you're writing software for avionics or nuclear power plants, there's a grueling review process before you can ship. You know how most software comes with an end user license agreement that basically says the software has no warranty and may blow up at any moment? In avionics, there's no such easy way out—people's lives really do depend on your code.

For the rest of us, however, there's no One True Way to do reviews. The best policy reviews code when it'll do the most good, and that varies based on the team and the project. (Tip: the answer is never "never.") An experienced manager or technical lead should set policy as needed.

Regardless, *you* can always call a review. When you want extra eyes on your code, ask without shame. Experienced programmers do it all the time. When a junior programmer doesn't ask for reviews, that's a certain sign of trouble brewing.

Actions

Take the initiative for your next code review: ask someone to buddy the next set of changes you want to check into your team's code base. But before you grab a buddy, do a little homework:

1. Generate the list of files you've changed. The source control system should tell you this readily; it's usually the status command.

2. Pull up diffs for each file, preferably in a graphical diff tool that lets you see both the original copy and your copy with the changes highlighted.

3. Now, don't skip this step, *look through the changes yourself,* and make sure you can explain every one of them. I'm not talking about an audit-style drill-down on your motivation for every line of code, but look for obvious goofs. There's also a good chance you left some cruft in there on accident; fix that and pull new diffs.

Now grab a buddy. If your team doesn't do this by policy, just ask another programmer—preferably someone senior to you—something like, "Would you mind looking over my changes before I check them in?"

With your buddy nearby and the diffs on-screen, explain the objective for your changes, and then walk through the diffs for each file. You can drive or the buddy can, whatever works best. Assuming you program with decent style (and why wouldn't you?), the buddy should be able to scan your changes quickly.

In addition to explaining the code, explain how you tested it. Ideally you have an automated unit test suite; review this code too. If not, explain any testing you did by hand or any reasoning about the correctness of your code.

Chances are you'll catch a couple goofs before you even call your buddy over. Plus, your buddy will ask a question or two you hadn't thought of. You may find that you want a check-in buddy for *every* commit.

CHAPTER 2

Get Your Tools in Order

Tools don't make a programmer great any more than a fancy guitar makes a guitarist great. Put me on the fanciest guitar you can find, and I'll make it sound like a washtub full of cats. But have you noticed that most great guitarists still have swank gear?

Great programmers are passionate about their tools in the same way. The right tools *multiply* the productivity of a great programmer. If you have the skills and a small effort can crank up your output to eleven, you'd be crazy not to take advantage of it, right?

This chapter introduces tools common to all software work. The time you invest in considering each tool discussed here will repay itself many, many times over during your career. You should also keep the same openness of mind in the years ahead; new tools will be created that may serve you better, or your career may take you into specialized realms where a different tool is better suited to the work.

- Tip 9, *Optimize Your Environment*, on page 61 starts us off by making the most of your day-to-day tools.

- Next we step back and consider the source code itself: Tip 10, *Speak Your Language Fluently*, on page 69 focuses on polishing your use of programming languages.

- One more step back: Tip 11, *Know Your Platform*, on page 77 looks at the whole software (even hardware) stack.

- Sometimes slacking is good. In Tip 12, *Automate Your Pain Away*, on page 83, we make the computer help out.

Productivity Multipliers vs. Dividers

I talk a lot about multiplying your productivity by using tools better. However, there's a trap that programmers can fall into: endlessly fiddling with their tools instead of getting work done. I've seen elaborate setups with virtual desktops, integrated development environments, remote file replication, and all kinds of mess that never seems to work quite right—yet the programmer keeps fiddling with it when he would be much better off if he'd run vi and *just start programming*.

With any plan to multiply your productivity, you need to draw a line in the sand; at some point, if it's not delivering, scrap it and move on. Keep in mind this balance: what's the fancy, productivity-multiplying solution? And what's the simplest thing that could possibly work? Give the fancy solution a fixed amount of time, and if that time expires, revert to simple.

- Tip 13, *Control Time (and Timelines)*, on page 87 introduces the version control system to help manage code across time and among programmers.

- Finally, sometimes it's best if you *don't* do the work yourself. Tip 14, *Use the Source, Luke*, on page 92 talks about integrating open source software with your commercial projects.

Tip 9

Optimize Your Environment

 [*White Belt*]   You use your development tools every day. Take a mental step back—the choices you made years ago may not be the best going forward.

Let's start at the beginning: when it's time to work, what program do you start? Visual Studio, Emacs, a terminal window? Before you ever get to writing code, you have the *environment* you program in. Your environment includes your computer, text editor, compiler, debugger, and so forth.

Chances are you're using only a fraction of the capabilities offered by each of these tools. You can make big gains in efficiency with just modest investment.

Text Editor

A co-worker of mine who's a machinist taunts programmers: "You have the easiest job in the world; it's just typing." Indeed, we *do* spend a lot of time typing. There are some other details involved, of course—programmers have an odd aversion to vowels and a special fondness for semi-colons—but sometimes your bottleneck truly is getting characters on-screen.

Given all the time you spend typing, if you could make the text editor do some of the tedious work for you—maybe save 10 percent of your effort—can you imagine how much that saves over the course of a year?

If you watch a master programmer at work, the first thing you'll notice is not the wizardry of their code; it'll be their wizardry of *manipulating* their code. The master seemingly types ahead of the computer, because even as they zap code from one place to another in an instant, they're thinking five steps ahead and could, quite literally, close their eyes for a few seconds and let their fingers catch up.

Integrated Development Environments

Products like Visual Studio and Eclipse put a bunch of tools under a single user interface. The *integrated development environment* (IDE) has its advantages; primarily, it's easy to pick up and use. Don't let an IDE limit your exploration, however. Discrete tools, like Vim for text editing, have staying power among programmers because they're tremendously powerful. The discussion in this tip applies regardless of using an IDE or separate tools.

The Programmer's Editor

This ability to blaze through code requires, first, a *programmer's* editor. There are plenty of these to go around, from primitive-looking vi to fancy-pants TextMate. No matter what generation you choose, common properties of a good editor include the following:

- Keyboard-heavy operation. The mouse is optional. *Learn the keyboard shortcuts* for common operations because it's a lot faster than constantly reaching for the mouse. This is why the old-school Unix editors are still popular; they make very good use of the keyboard. (If you think this is just for programmers, consider that any graphic designer worth their salt knows the keyboard shortcuts for Adobe Photoshop and Illustrator by heart. They work with one hand on the keyboard and the other on a graphic tablet.)

- Complex movement and selection tools. A programmer's editor is smart enough to move among not just lines and columns but also logical blocks of code. With the cursor on a block, you should be able to select the block and move it with just a few keystrokes. And again, hands off the mouse.

- Language-aware syntax highlighting. For some, this helps to see the "bigger picture" of the code that's on-screen; others don't care. If nothing else, it makes your code look a lot fancier so that snooty machinists think you're doing something more than mere typing.

- Language-aware indentation. There's no reason to hit the spacebar a bunch of times to indent each line; a good editor will assist you with indentation rules that match your programming language and preferred style.

- Text completion. Once you've typed a long variable or function name, there's no reason to type it again. A programmer's editor will allow you to type part of the name and hit a key to autocomplete the rest. (Where the part you typed is ambiguous, usually hitting the auto-complete key repeatedly will cycle through possible matches.)

The second key to blazing through code is simple: put in your time. Fancy editors take a long time to learn, so set aside a little time each week to learn a new trick. You can't do it all at once, because you need to get the tricks into your *muscle memory.* This means it's instinctive; your fingers do the actions automatically without your conscious mind involved—your conscious mind stays focused on the code.

Finally, watch some of your senior peers at their editors. Do some pair programming with them driving, and as soon as you think, "I didn't even know you could *do* that!" take a note and figure out how they did it.

Editing Over SSH

It's common in a programmer's workday that you need to access a remote machine through a simple SSH, serial, or other text-only console. You need to learn the basics of one editor that can run in text-only mode. It doesn't really matter how many tricks you can make your GUI editor do when you're on another machine at a console prompt.

For this purpose, I recommend vi.[1] vi is on any Unix-like machine you'll walk up to. Others (notably Emacs) may or may not be there. Therefore, if nothing else, spend an hour learning enough vi to make simple changes. It'll pay off the next time you have a server that's half-dead and only bootable to a single-user console.

---

1. On many modern systems vi is actually Vim—*vi improved*—which has additional features.

Language Tools

We'll discuss programming languages in Tip 10, *Speak Your Language Fluently,* on page 69, but for the moment let's briefly consider the tools that are part of your environment. These commonly include compilers, debuggers, or interpreters. In an IDE, there's usually a button for *build* that invokes the build system, usually compiling code. Whatever it is, learn the keyboard shortcuts, and don't go hunting for the mouse every time you need to build.

Some languages don't have compilers; they are interpreted, and they often have a Read, Evaluate, Print Loop (REPL) that lets you type expressions and print the result immediately. The REPL is an essential time-saver because you can get quick answers to questions without needing to run your whole program. For example, if you need to do some fancy transformations on data, pop open the REPL and try them with some sample data.

Some environments integrate the development tools in novel ways. First, they may bring the REPL into your text editor and allow you to take the current line, evaluate it using the language interpreter, and print the results right in the same window. Talk about immediate gratification.

Second, some environments include language-aware refactoring features that let you (for example) rename a method and also rename all calls to the method. Behind the scenes, the environment is constantly compiling or interpreting your program so it refactors with real smarts—not just a global search and replace.

Debuggers

Many environments include a source-level debugger. This allows you to stop program execution—by crash or by choice—and inspect the state of the program, such as the call stack or values of variables. In a language like C where a crash is typified with the unhelpful message "segmentation fault," a debugger is essential to getting even basic information about a crash. Fancier languages will usually dump the call stack, which may be all you need to identify the problem.

Debuggers tend to come with a price—they slow down execution of the program. This can cause timing-related problems to pop up or go away. These are affectionately known as *Heisenbugs,* bugs that you can either experience or try to debug, but not both at the same time.

Depending on your platform, the debugger may be helpful in doing post-mortem analysis, too. With C programs on Linux, for example, a crash can generate a *core file,* which includes a dump of system memory. The debugger can load the core file and tell you the state of threads and variables at the time of the crash. (The term *core* refers to magnetic core memory, an early form of RAM that hasn't been in use since the 1970s. The term is still used to refer to RAM in general.)

If you're good at writing unit tests, chances are you won't need the debugger much; you'll catch most bugs with your tests. Bugs of the simple *duh!* variety are easy to test. However, some classes of bugs—especially those dealing with timing of IO or threads—are extremely hard to catch with automated tests. For those, hope for a good core file or stack trace.

Profiling

What about situations where the program is technically correct but too slow? Knuth wrote, "Premature optimization is the root of all evil." To this end, write your code to be *correct* first. If you have a performance problem, *measure* the problem before trying to fix it.

This is what a profiler does: it tells you how many times each function is called and how much time is spent in each function. The results will often surprise you. For example, I profiled a toy Sudoku solver of mine and discovered it spending most of its time iterating over its list of cells. A small bit of caching made it run 3,000 times faster.

The most baffling performance problems are when your program is just *sitting there* and doing nothing most of the time. This can occur when there's contention for a resource; the profiler will show your program spending a lot of time in the function used to lock the resource. Or it may show that the problem isn't in your program at all—perhaps it's a network resource that's slow, and the profiler will show your program waiting in the network receive function.

Actions

Fortunately, you won't have any problem trying development environments—you use one every day. However, focused practice can help you get more out of your environment.

Text Editor Tricks

As mentioned, you need to do this one over time so you can build muscle memory. Commit to learning one new trick a week.

- Learn to move between files with only the keyboard. Bonus points if your environment is smart enough to know some relations between files, such as hopping between application code and its unit tests. Then learn to navigate quickly within a file: by page, by function, by block of code. Then within a line: beginning and end, word by word.

- Learn to select the current line and current code block. For editors that have multiple clipboards, learn to cut and paste more than one thing at a time. (In Emacs this is known as the *kill ring*.)

- You can usually spare some typing with autocomplete features. These may be language-aware; for example, your editor may know the standard library functions and allow you to select one from a list as you start typing. Others will allow you to complete a word based on other text in the file, which is just as handy. Learn these shortcuts; they're a tremendous time-saver.

- Most editors can auto-indent your code. Turn this on, configure it for your style, and say goodbye to your Tab key.

Compiler/Interpreter Tricks

- The first trick is turning on warnings, a feature offered by most programming compilers or interpreters. These warnings aren't always bugs, but you should check each one to be sure—then fix the code to eliminate the warning. (In legacy code this isn't always an option, but try when you can. "Warning spew" just causes programmers to ignore warnings, and you could miss something important.)

- For projects with a build/compile step, learn the keyboard shortcut for building your project.

- When there are compile warnings or errors, they come with a file and line number. Learn the keyboard shortcut to hop to the source code indicated by the current error.

- If your language has a REPL, learn the keyboard shortcut to start it.

- If your environment has refactoring features, learn the keyboard shortcuts for renaming a method, renaming a class, and extracting a block of code into its own method.

Debugger Tricks

- Learn the keyboard shortcut for starting your program in the debugger.

- Get a stack trace from a program crash. This shows the nesting of functions and answers the essential question, "How did I get here?"

- Set a breakpoint in your source code, and then run the debugger and get there. Breakpoints are essential when investigating a problem *before* the program crashes.

- If your platform supports core files, learn how to turn them on. Force a crash to generate a core file, and then load that into the debugger.

Profiler Tricks

You don't need the profiler often, but you should know how to run it and interpret the results.

- Programmers love sorting algorithms. Implement a couple of list sorts—don't forget bogosort[2]—and run them with 10, 100, and 1,000 (or more) elements under

---

2.   http://en.wikipedia.org/wiki/Bogosort

the profiler. As the number of elements increases, you should be able to clearly see the difference in execution time between the algorithms. (Bonus points if you can determine the order of growth—Big-O—for each algorithm based on your data for number of elements vs. execution time.)

Tip 10

Speak Your Language Fluently

 *[White Belt]* You get paid to tell the computer what to do, so you'd best tell it as effectively as possible.

As programmers, we are translators in a way: we take a description of a program expressed in human languages and translate it to a real program expressed in a programming language. Translators must be fluent in both languages to be effective.

Fluency in programming languages is somewhat ill-defined, however. Many books purport to teach you, for example, Java in 21 days. I've even seen one that claims to teach Java in 24 hours. Perhaps you could learn the syntax of Java and some of its library calls, but would you call yourself *fluent* after 24 hours, or even 21 days? No way.

No Shortcuts

A language—or any skill for that matter—takes about 10,000 hours of dedicated practice to reach true competency. Malcolm Gladwell[3] and Peter Norvig[4] both make a compelling case for the 10,000-hour rule. This works out to about ten years for most people.

Within those ten years, the mastery curve looks like Figure 2, *Language/platform learning curve*, on page 70. There's a couple notable points. First, you won't get far past "Hello World" without hitting a wall of frustration. That's normal; there's a base of knowledge you need to assimilate—syntax, libraries, and such—in order to be productive at all. Past that, you hit a plateau of competency where you can putter along and pay the bills but you're not great. This is the long grind where you're cutting the grooves in your mind so that

---

3. *Outliers: The Story of Success* [Gla08]
4. http://norvig.com/21-days.html

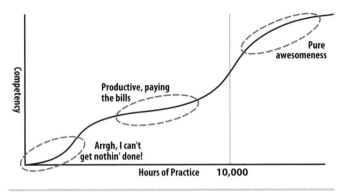

Figure 2—Language/platform learning curve

you can truly *think* in that language. If you stick with it, your competency starts taking off again as you reach toward true mastery.

There's value in sticking with one language, or a set of related languages, through the 10,000-hour mark. With every additional language, you increase your skill as a programmer across the board, but you need to take at least *one* past 10,000 hours. Consider, by contrast, 1,000 hours of practice in 10 languages: how effective would you be at your job as a beginner in 10 languages?

By the same accord, you need to keep challenging yourself to make those 10,000 hours count. It's easy to keep yourself challenged at first—*everything* is a challenge early on—but some people get stuck on that early plateau. Consider the website programmer who builds a site with a shopping cart, then another, then another…twenty web sites later, he's paying the bills OK, but is he actually *learning* anything?

Andy Hunt writes in *Pragmatic Thinking and Learning* [Hun08] that practice requires a well-defined task that's challenging but doable, feedback on how you're doing, and the chance to repeat the task (or a similar one) and do better. Many places I've worked are good at all but the feedback part. As in Tip 8, *Review Code Early and Often*, on page 53, seek out feedback from senior programmers early on to ensure you keep learning.

Related Languages

Some skills carry over from one language to another. You can argue, for example, that C++ and Java take a similar approach to object-oriented programming. Thus, time spent in either one counts toward your 10,000-hour mark in OOP skill. However, only C++ counts toward your "adventures with pointers" skill.

There are many subskills wrapped up in learning a programming language; thus, the 10,000-hour rule is fuzzier in practice than it sounds in principle.

Idiomatic Programming

Once you get past the initial learning curve of a language's syntax, you get into learning its *style*, or its *idiom*. There's a maxim that "a good C programmer can write C in any language." I've seen it happen—and in my younger years have been guilty of it myself. What the maxim is getting at is, if you only ever think in terms of C programming, you miss the different ways of thinking that other languages can offer.

For example, consider the following code snippets that all add the numbers in a list. First there's C and the classic for loop:

```
SumArray.c
int a[] = {1, 2, 3, 4, 5};
int sum = 0;

for (int i = 0; i < sizeof(a) / sizeof(int); i++) {
    sum += a[i];
}
```

You *could* write largely the same thing in Ruby, but that's not *idiomatic* Ruby. In Ruby, you use a block for this kind of thing:

```
SumArray.rb
sum = 0

[1, 2, 3, 4, 5].each do |i|
  sum += i
end
```

But even that's not truly idiomatic Ruby. The better way is to use Enumerable.inject, which abstracts the concept of combining all elements of a collection:

```
SumArray.rb
sum = [1, 2, 3, 4, 5].inject(:+)
```

In the same way, C programmers think of chewing through an array in terms of for loops, Ruby programmers think in terms of blocks, and Lisp and Scheme programmers think in terms of recursion. Here's what the same code would look like in Scheme (without the reduce shortcut):

```
SumArray.scheme
(define (sum-array a)
  (if (null? a)
     0
     (+ (car a) (sum-array (cdr a)))))

(sum-array (list 1 2 3 4 5))
```

The idiom of a language moves you toward *thinking* about your program in the way the language's designers intended. In languages that are conceptually similar (say, C++ and Java) many idioms are shared where the language's features overlap. With totally different languages (like C and Scheme shown earlier), you truly need to change your thinking.

There are a couple ways to learn idiomatic programming: first, if there's a great book on the language, by all means start there; for C that could be *The C Programming Language* [KR98], and for Scheme I'd read *Structure and Interpretation of Computer Programs* [AS96]. Study the examples and study *why* the author writes the code the way they do.

Second, find open source projects written in the language and study them. This can be tricky, because the quality of code in the wild varies wildly. It can range from stupid and buggy to wizardly and incomprehensible. A good resource for small, straightforward code samples is the Rosetta Code[5] website.

Balance Your Productivity with the Machine's

Programmers often measure their mettle by how fast they can make a program run or how small they can make it. An often repeated example is Andy Hertzfeld rewriting a puzzle game in 1983 from a 6,000-byte Pascal program to a 600-byte

---

5.   http://rosettacode.org

assembly language program.[6] This is good fun—for a sufficiently geeky definition of "fun"—and sometimes essential to the job.

Where trouble starts is when programmers think they need to write *all* programs fast and small. More often than not, the computer's efficiency is less important than *your* efficiency. Computers are cheap. Programmers are expensive. It's therefore a better bet to program using a high-level language and in a clear, straightforward manner.

This is part of why languages like Ruby and Python have become tremendously popular: they allow the programmer to write programs quickly. As long as the program runs fast enough, who cares if it takes longer to run than an assembly language program?

Even Andy Hertzfeld's story follows this model: he first wrote his puzzle game in Pascal, the highest-level language available on the Macintosh at that time. He wrote the assembly version only when he *needed* it smaller.

There are some cases, however, where the computer should trump the programmer:

- Any program that is too slow and can't be fixed by adding more machines. Some problems can be fixed by running more machines in parallel. (Most web applications fall into this category.) But other problems are inherently sequential. In the latter case, when the sequential part is too slow, you have to rewrite it to go faster.

- Data sets that can grow to unbounded sizes. When you're developing a program, you usually test with small data sets so everything fits in memory (possibly even cache) and runs great. If the real-world use of the program could include huge data sets, your design must account for that.

- Anything in the operating system. System calls get called constantly, and interrupts fire constantly, and it's the operating system's job to service them quickly and return control to applications.

---

6.   http://www.folklore.org/StoryView.py?story=Puzzle.txt

Finally, consider the case where some of your program is bound by the computer's efficiency but most of it is not. Who says all of your program must be written in the same language? The use of *hybrid* designs is becoming popular. Games, for example, have extreme demands on the machine for their graphics, physics, and audio—this stuff is usually written in C. Games also have a lot of "world logic" like how a switch responds to the player pressing it. There's no reason to write the latter in C. Many games have started using languages like Lua for their world logic because it's more efficient for the game designers to work with.[7]

Competitive Advantage

You've probably noticed a trend: despite the desire to achieve competency in one programming language, you'll need to learn more than one in your career. In part, this is because the world keeps moving: the generally accepted languages will change, and you, to be effective, will need to follow. In part this is because you should diversify; a programmer who can work in several languages will find more work than a one-trick pony.

Mastery of at least one low-level language and one high-level language will give you tremendous professional flexibility. In some situations you're machine-bound, and you'll need the machine efficiency of a language like C to make the program efficient enough. In other situations you're programmer-bound, and the increased efficiency of a language like Ruby will help you get the program written quickly.

This all boils down to using the right tool for the job. With several tools at your disposal, you have an advantage over others who stubbornly try to bludgeon every problem into submission using whatever language they learned first. This requires you to learn more—usually on your own time—but it pays off by making you a more effective programmer.

---

7. http://lua-users.org/wiki/LuaUses

Actions

Well, the 10,000-hour part is going to take a while, isn't it? For now, let's focus on your options: take the programming language you know now and one or two that you're curious about. For best effect, pick languages with very different idioms.

Beyond "Hello World"

First, let's *not* write a program that prints "Hello World" to the console. (Well, OK, I bet you already did. "Hello" back.) Here's your first program: read a file that has an integer on each line. Print the minimum, maximum, mean, and median of the data set. Why? This exercises several basic principles common to many computing tasks: working with IO, iterating over a collection, and doing a little math.

The key goal is to not just make some code work but to write the program *in the idiom* of the language. As a secondary goal, try this in a test-driven style. For example, you'll need a function that returns the median of a collection. Write some sample tests for that before writing the actual function. Test-driven development is discussed further in Tip 2, *Insist on Correctness*, on page 11.

Sudoku

Ben Laurie comments, Sudoku is "a denial-of-service attack on the human intellect."[8] That may be so, but it's also a fun programming puzzle. You need to reason about data, constraints, and search heuristics.

Your task is to write a program that can read a Sudoku grid from a file—with some cells filled in and others blank—and then solve the puzzle and print the result. You can find puzzles online; just search for *easy sudoku* and so forth. Start with an easy puzzle; the generally accepted standard of *easy* is that it can be solved without guessing. This should test your solver's ability to apply the rules of the game.

When you have the rules established, move onto hard puzzles. You'll need to search (guess) to solve the puzzle, and

---

8. http://norvig.com/sudoku.html—but don't go looking here, try to solve it yourself first!

your choice of search heuristic will have a dramatic impact on the performance of the solver. This is a good opportunity to apply the scientific method: make a hypothesis about a heuristic, and then measure its performance vs. another.

The point of this exercise is partly to give your brain a workout but to also give you a program sufficiently large that idiomatic use of the language starts to pay off—if you're on the right track, it should *feel* like you're using the language right; if you're not, it should feel like you're fighting the language. In the latter case, try to find an expert (in-person or online) to help.

Tip 11

Know Your Platform

 [*Brown Belt*] For your first job, you'll focus on one platform, but over time you'll need to pick up more.

When most programmers think about development tools, they immediately think about the programming language. That's only half the picture: the language is part of a larger computing *platform*. Consider the olden days when computers were programmed only in assembly language; each type of computer had its own instruction set, so depending on your application, some computers could offer better instructions than others.

The same is true today. Consider Java: it's not just a programming language; it's a language *and* a set of standard libraries *and* a virtual machine to deploy your application on, as illustrated in Figure 3, *Java software stack*, on page 79. These layers underneath your program are called the *platform*—it's like the foundation of a house. Java is a platform as much as it is a language. (In fact, there are other languages like Scala and Clojure that run on the Java platform, too.)

The platform stack goes all the way down to the hardware and possibly further to the network and storage infrastructure as well. How far you need to think depends on your application. Google, for example, needs to think all the way down to how it distributes data centers across the world—as of this writing, they build Lego-style data centers in shipping containers that they can drop anywhere they can get enough power and network bandwidth.[9]

Chances are you don't need to fill shipping containers with thousands of computers. But what if you need to, say, store some data and query it later? Common problem. You could

---

9.   US Patent 7,738,251

solve it with in-memory data structures, flat files on disk, an embedded database, an external network database...you get the idea. You need another component in your platform, and your decision affects your product as dramatically as your choice of programming language.

Platform Investment

Platforms require investment in the same way as programming languages, both from the individual and from the organization. At the individual level, it takes time to learn each part of the stack and how they all interact. At the organizational level, there's fiscal investment, deployed software (either in the field or in the data center), and a whole bunch of programmers who are familiar with the platform. Because of this, it pays to take an economic view of platforms. The usual investing advice is to do your research and diversify.

On the research front, you can't base a decision solely on reading a few web pages; you can always find ten pages that say component x rocks and another ten that say it sucks. You need to do some firsthand investigation to see how well each component works for you in your situation.

Then there's diversification: research multiple options, and keep your design as modular as possible. Down the road you may need to switch out your database, change languages, or otherwise rip up and rework. The Internet is a good example of modular design and diversification at work. The standards for protocols like TCP, IP, and HTTP were written so any computer could implement them; therefore, *every* computer implemented them. This allowed Internet protocols to flourish, and many vendor-unique protocols died off.

Here are a few practical ways to choose platforms. First, come up with three possible options and set aside a fixed amount of time to try each. Setting aside the time is essential, because it removes the pressure to solve the problem perfectly from the start—you *know* that you'll throw away two options. At the end you've prototyped your solution several different ways, you know a lot more about the problem domain, and you can make an informed decision about the best way to proceed.

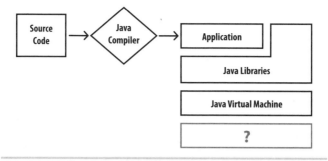

Figure 3—Java software stack

Second, make interfaces between components as generic as possible. For example, when exchanging data between components, consider using a generic format like XML or JSON instead of a custom binary format. The generic format is much easier to parse using a variety of languages and allows for easier change down the road.

Actions

Let's consider a handful of platforms and how to get started in each. You'll notice big differences in the workflow and programming style they demand. If possible, find a mentor who knows the platforms and who can help you program idiomatically.

Warm-up: Console Interface

First, get the program logic into shape on the simplest possible platform, a console application. This requires only one program file and no GUI beyond printf(). You can pick any language you like, but I'll discuss C.

The objective is the classic Fahrenheit/Celsius converter. Feel free to do something fancier. Here's a quick specification:

- The user should be able to specify the conversion as command-line arguments, -c (degrees Celsius) or -f (degrees Fahrenheit).

- The user should be able to specify the conversion as command-line arguments, -c (degrees Celsius) or -f (degrees Fahrenheit).

- If no arguments are supplied, the program should prompt the user for degrees and unit.

- If the user provides arguments that cannot be converted meaningfully (non-numeric, out of range), the program needs to detect that and print an appropriate message.

This is mostly a warm-up exercise so you don't get bogged down in the platform itself, but even a simple console application is built on a platform. In this case, it's your C compiler and the C standard library. On Unix-like platforms, you can display your application's dependencies with this:

```
ldd [program]
```

You should see something like libc. This is a *shared library* that's used to provide the C standard library for all programs running on your machine.

Desktop GUI

From here things can diverge quickly depending on your preferred operating system. Windows, Mac OS, Linux, and others evolved with separate GUI programming interfaces, so creating a *native* application means learning a separate toolkit for each. (In the case of Mac OS, it requires learning a new programming language, too: Objective-C.)

There are also ways to create *cross-platform* GUI programs using a framework like Qt[10] or a platform like Java.

Here's a specification for your GUI temperature converter:

- The program should display a window with a text field, a drop-down box for conversion, and a second text field for the conversion result.

- The first text field should be editable but allow only digits, decimal points, and plus/minus signs.

- The second text field should not be editable; it should be used only for the program's display.

- If the temperature entered is out of range, an error dialog should tell the user why and then clamp the entered value to the closest valid temperature.

---

10. http://qt.nokia.com

- (Bonus points) The conversion result field should update as the user types each character.

- In your code, separate the conversion code from the code that's handling the GUI widgets and events.

The first thing to note is there's no main() function where you're waiting for the user to type something. Instead, you get *events* from on-screen widgets when the user clicks or types something. This style of programming will probably feel strange because you're not driving the program flow; the user is.

The second thing to note is the two-step processes where you build the graphical part of the GUI first and then add the code that makes it go. In geek terms, this is separating the *view* from the *model*. (The model is all your "business logic," which in this case isn't much.)

Model/view separation[11] becomes very important in large projects, because the model is often used from multiple places. Imagine a commerce application where orders are coming in from point-of-sale terminals, shipping is pulling orders out with their own application, and accounting is pulling reports using a third application. There are three views, but only one model is needed.

Web

The beauty of web applications is that you have a standard presentation layer (HTML, CSS, JavaScript) and a standard means of communicating with a server (HTTP). The ugly side is that these technologies were originally created for *pages* and not *applications*, so building your fancy web app tends to involve a lot of late nights and cold pizza.

Web applications are here to stay, of course. It's easy to get a basic form on a page and then create a back-end server that can both vend the page and accept a form submission. That's what we'll do.

The specification is very similar to the previous desktop GUI case. However, I will add the following:

---

11. http://en.wikipedia.org/wiki/Model-view-controller

- The form should live on one page only, both for its initial state and after the conversion.

- The temperature conversion must be done on the server, not using JavaScript in the web browser.

- Do this first using a form and a submit button.

- (Bonus points) Instead of submitting the form, respond to the user typing in the text field and update the conversion using JavaScript and XMLHttpRequest (aka XHR or Ajax). Again, the conversion should come from the server.

The first wall people run into with web applications is that *all requests are independent*. That means you cannot assume that subsequent requests to your web server are coming from the same user. You cannot assume the user will go to a page you redirected them to. They can type anything in their browser's URL bar they please, and they can simply leave your site, too.

The next problem you hit is usually complexity. Vending one page is easy; vending a hundred turns into a real mess if you don't structure your application well. That's when you're best off with a framework like Ruby on Rails. Such frameworks have a large up-front learning curve. What you get in return is a modular system that can grow in complexity and scale to large traffic loads.

In all these scenarios, we've only scratched the surface of what each platform can do; you could collect a whole shelf of books on each one if you decide to go further. I hope you've gotten a taste of each type of platform and where to go to learn more.

Tip 12

Automate Your Pain Away

 [*White Belt*] You can start automating tasks for yourself no matter what your role or how your project is structured. (Plus, it's a given that newbies will be given some mundane tasks—exactly the kind of tasks that beg for automation.)

In any industry project, the program build is automated, so you just need to type make or click a button. The tools used for compiling source code, however, are generic automation tools; they can be used for a lot more than running compilers. Like many of the topics we've discussed, automation is a productivity multiplier—use it well, and the time invested up front multiplies your effort later.

There's a famous Despair.com de-motivational poster that says, "If a pretty poster and a cute saying are all it takes to motivate you, you probably have a very easy job. The kind robots will be doing soon.[12]" If a robot can do the job you're doing, then either you should make the robot or someone else will. Your value as a programmer is in your *thinking*, not your typing.

Automatic and Repeatable

The goal of automation is twofold: to eliminate tedium and to give you repeatable results. On the tedium side, there are a lot of steps in a programmer's workflow that look like this:

1. When someone changes a file in the version control system (see Tip 13, *Control Time (and Timelines)*, on page 87), then the installer package needs to be rebuilt.

2. When the package changes, it should be deployed to the test servers.

---

12. http://despair.com/motivation.html

3. When a test server gets a new package, it should kill the running application process and start the one in the new package.

4. *...and so on.*

How many times do you need to run these commands by hand before you want to pull your hair out? As it turns out, computers are great at these kinds of tasks. You can use hooks in your source control system to trigger the package build. Deploying the package should be as simple as copying it to a network repository and telling the repository to update itself. Restarting the application on each server could be a step in the package's post-install process.

Any time one action naturally follows another, you have an opportunity for automation. Use your thinking to spare yourself the typing.

Automation Reduces Error

Automation isn't just about eliminating tedium from your day; it's also about reducing error. There's a rule in programming that you should eliminate duplicate code wherever possible, because inevitably someone will change one part of the code and forget to change the other. The same is true of processes. Let's say you must increment a version number each time you build a package; inevitably someone will build the package but forget to increment the version number. Now you have two packages floating around that are different yet have identical versions.

Obviously, the way to eliminate this error is to make the process automatic. The computer, when told it must increment the version each time it does a package build, will repeatedly demonstrate its ability to follow orders.

Actions

The best automation tool depends entirely on the job you're trying to automate. However, there are a few common tasks that every programmer gets saddled with.

Build
> (*examples: Ant, Maven, Make, Rake*) These are dependency-driven tools that are mostly used for compiling code.

Generally, C programs use make, and Java programs use ant or Maven, but there are no strict rules—the tools are general purpose.

Starting with the tool your company uses, create a simple project from scratch and learn to automate some tasks. For example, with C or Java, make a dependency rule that automatically compiles files when they change. Make a test target (make test or similar) that depends on all files being compiled and then runs unit tests. Finally, make a documentation target that runs JavaDoc—or whatever is appropriate—to create doc files.

You'll notice that targets can have dependencies—for example, unit tests require that all source files are compiled—and the tool will recurse as necessary to fulfill them in the correct order.

Packaging

(examples: RPM, APT, InstallShield) Each operating system has its favored packaging system, and it's usually an uphill battle to do your own thing, so don't. Packaging is mundane, but it's a tremendous time-saver when you need to deploy code. Further, its automatic dependency resolution can save you from a whole host of errors.

Pick a packaging system and make a simple "Hello World" application. Then package your application for distribution. If you're on Linux, for example, make the package install your app to /usr/bin/hello. Now for some fun (for a very nerdy definition of "fun"). First, install and uninstall your package. The application should get removed when the package is uninstalled.

Install your package again. Next, increment the version of your package and move the install target, for example, to /usr/local/bin/hello. Now upgrade to the new version of the package. Your old application should go away, and the new one should be in its correct spot.

Finally, use your build automation tool to create the package for you. Now you can use one command to go from source code to a deployable package. Cool, huh?

System Administration

(examples: too many to list) Buy a book on system administration; you're guaranteed to find a lot of things your operating system can do to relieve burden. On Unix, cron can run tasks at regular intervals, ssh can run commands on remote systems, find can find new or stale files for you, and so forth. Learn ten new commands over the next two weeks.

Control Time (and Timelines)

 [*White Belt*] Good version control is central to a good daily workflow. It's an essential organizational tool, and even better, it lets you answer the age-old question, "Where the heck did this code come from?"

The purpose of a version control system is simple: it tracks some content (generally files) over time, allowing you to commit new versions of content and roll back to previous versions. A competent system will also track multiple timelines and assist with merging content between them. With a basic understanding of how this works, it's a *tremendously* useful tool—one that you'll wonder how you ever lived without.

Moving Through Time

There are a couple reasons you need to move back in time with your source code—and any content, for that matter. First, you may screw up and need to revert to a previous version. It's a fact of life; sometimes you'll work yourself into a mess, and the easiest path is simply to throw away your last day of work and start over. A version control system allows you to do this easily.

Second, when you release code, you need the ability go back and look at what you released. It's entirely normal for problems to crop up in the field that you need to fix but without changing anything else. Thus, you need to stash your current work, check out the released code, and make a fix on that copy. Then you'll want to merge that fix to your in-progress code.

To move through time, you need to tell the version control system when to take a snapshot of your work. This is known as a *commit*. Usually you'll have a batch of changes, and they'll all get committed together as one version. If needed, you can revert your changes or simply pull another copy of the source code at any prior version.

When a version represents a milestone you want to refer to later, for example a product release, you assign a *tag* to that version. This is simply a convenient name that you can refer to later. When you check out the released version of code, you can specify the tag name instead of the version number.

Coordinating with Others

Programming is a group effort, and the version control system is your hub for coordinating efforts on a shared code base. When others have committed code, you'll update your version to incorporate their changes. This is called a *merge* operation, where two variants of a file are used to create a new version incorporating all changes. Most of the time the version control system will merge your co-workers' changes with yours automatically.

Sometimes two programmers will be working on the same code, and their work will overlap. One lucky programmer will need to manually merge the overlapping changes. The version control system will mark overlapping changes in the file, one section for the upstream changes and another for your changes, and you edit the file to make it right.

Multiple Timelines

The final basic practice of version control is managing multiple timelines. The classic case goes like this: you release version 1.0 of your product and start working on features for 2.0. Customers report bugs, and you need to create a bug-fix release to 1.0 without introducing the 2.0 changes. Therefore, you create two parallel timelines in the version control system: one for 1.0 bug fixes and another for 2.0 features.

Traditionally, the feature development timeline is called the *trunk*, and the others are called *branches*. This is because the trunk always continues on, whereas branches tend to have a limited life span. If you plotted the relationships over time, they'd have a treelike appearance with the trunk running through the center.

There are two traditional uses for branches: first, as we mentioned, is to control changes that go into a released version of code. This is, unsurprisingly, called a *release branch*. The second use is for more speculative feature development that is considered too risky to do on the trunk. These *feature branches* are developed to a point of good-enough stability and then merged back to the trunk.

Centralized vs. Distributed

Version control systems have split into two competing philosophies about who's in charge of your content. Traditionally, systems have been client/server, and the server has the definitive copy of all content and its history. Clients can check out copies and commit new versions, but it's the server that's in charge of these transactions. Popular version control systems following this centralized model include Subversion and Perforce.

Another approach asserts that no one copy of the content is the master; instead, all clients contain the full version history so nobody (or *everybody*) is a definitive source. Popular systems following this decentralized model include Git and Mercurial.

I couldn't possibly address all the pros and cons of each approach here—that would require its own book—but I will say that the centralized approach is what you most often see in industry right now, and I expect this will be true for some time. Many programmers simply aren't comfortable with branching and merging on a frequent basis. (Distributed version control implies, to a degree, that every programmer has their own private branch.) However, these systems have much to offer for the team that learns to use them well.

Whichever type of system your company uses, master that first, including branch, merge, and tag operations. Then try your hand with a system from the other camp. As you learn, pay special attention to the *motivation* that drove the design of each type of system; they're not trying to solve exactly the same problem.

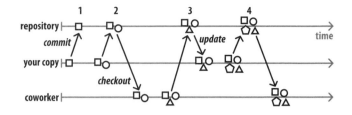

Figure 4—Version control: day-to-day collaboration

Actions

Learning version control isn't hard, but you do need to try concepts on a simple project before tackling big problems in the wild. Start with the system your company already uses. If you're on your own, pick any free VCS with good documentation—*Pragmatic Version Control Using Subversion* [Mas06] or *Pragmatic Version Control Using Git* [Swi08] would be a great starting point!

Fire up a terminal window and work through the following exercises with a simple code base:

Create Repository
> First, create a repository and add some files to it. This will be your master repository, and you're working on the trunk or default branch. Your first commit looks like the left side of Figure 4, *Version control: day-to-day collaboration*, on page 90.

Work on Trunk
> Make some changes and commit them. Now do a couple more commits. Get a log to show your history; it should include change-set (or revision) numbers and summaries of your changes. Update to a prior version—exercise your control over time.

Interact with a Co-worker
> Either borrow a co-worker or play along using two working trees. Make changes from both places and commit; if using a distributed system, pull changes from each other. Now we're at the right side of Figure 4, *Version control: day-to-day collaboration*, on page 90.

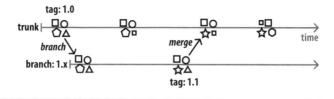

Figure 5—Version control: branch and merge

Change different files and watch the VCS automatically merge. See what happens when both you and your co-worker make a change to the same parts of a file and commit—you'll get a merge conflict you need to resolve.

Create a Branch

Let's say it's time to create a release to customers. Create a version 1.0 tag and a release branch, as in Figure 5, *Version control: branch and merge,* on page 91. You can choose to have two working copies of your project on disk, one for each branch, or just one copy that you can flip between the branch and the trunk.

Merge Branch to Trunk

Now change a file on the branch. Say this is release 1.1 and tag it. Merge the change back to the trunk using the version control system—you shouldn't have to do any copying and pasting.

Tip 14

Use the Source, Luke

[*Brown Belt*]   This could be white belt for you in the right company; in others, you need to build credibility before bringing in outside software.

Open source software is an essential building block of modern systems. You probably learned to program using open source development tools. Your cell phone is likely built using an open source kernel. Start-ups are building their businesses around open source, and even the old-guard tech companies like IBM are investing heavily in open source projects.

Other companies won't touch it. Open source presents a minefield of legal issues, most of which have never been tested in court.

Your company is probably somewhere in the middle, wanting to use a mix of open source and proprietary software, each to their best advantage. This gives you, as an individual programmer, several ways to build credibility and value within the company:

- With an awareness of the legal issues surrounding open source, you can give management all the license information they need to make educated decisions and reduce their legal risk.

- At the same time, you build their confidence that *you* won't get the company into legal trouble, nor give away company proprietary code on accident.

- By contributing improvements to open source projects, you reduce the company's ongoing code maintenance burden and build cred in the community.

- Many open source projects have quality standards that rival the best proprietary code. You'll learn a lot by playing at that level.

The focus of this tip is twofold. First you need grounding in the legal side so you don't get into trouble. Then we'll discuss workflow for a project that integrates open source software with a proprietary product.

Proprietary vs. Open

When a company chooses to keep its source code to itself—or said another way, they restrict others from using it—that's *proprietary* code. The company keeps the source code a secret, and users of the software get only compiled code.

Assuming you have a traditional employment contract, all code you write for the company is owned wholly by the company. Treat it as proprietary unless you're specifically told otherwise. Some companies have employment contracts that cover *all* code you write for the duration of your employment, even stuff done on your own time and with your own computer.

Open source code, on the other hand, is obviously posted in the open—but there are some less-obvious qualifications. Only *public domain* code is treated as having no owner; in other words, the person who wrote it formally gave up any rights of ownership.

Most open source code has a *copyright,* which is held by an individual or a company. Code should have a comment block at the top of each file that states the copyright holder. It'll look something like this (from FreeBSD):

```
/*
 * Copyright (c) 1989, 1993, 1994
 *      The Regents of the University of California.
 *      All rights reserved.
 *
 * Redistribution and use in source and binary forms,
 * with or without modification, are permitted provided
 * that the following conditions are met:
 * [...more here...]
 */
```

That means the copyright of the file is owned by UC, which has the exclusive right to determine the rules for how the file can be copied (or otherwise used). Immediately following are the rules they've chosen, known as the file's *license*.

(Note: you'll also hear the term *copyleft*,[13] but that's not actually a form of copyright—it's a philosophy of licensing.)

Licenses

Specific licenses change over time, and interpretations of licenses change as well. Many have not been tested in court. Therefore, I can't give specific advice—you'll need to consult your management, and possibly legal department, to determine which licenses are acceptable to your company.

For any license, you'll want to answer questions such as these:

- If you change any files covered by the license, does the license require that you openly publish your changes?
- If you add your own features in new files, are there any requirements that you make those changes public?
- If the licensed code contains any patented technologies, do you get a license to those patents?
- Does the license require you to put a copyright notice in your product or its documentation?

Fortunately, there are common licenses that are used by many open source projects. If you're looking to use a dozen open source components in your project, you may need to research only three or four licenses.

The GNU Public License (GPL) is especially problematic in commercial projects: it requires that all code linked to GPL code also be GPL. A company may not be willing to open source its own proprietary code under the GPL. You need to be *very* careful about how you use GPL code; many companies avoid the issue with a "no GPL code anywhere" policy.

---

13. http://www.gnu.org/copyleft/

> ## Warning: Turn Off Your Copy and Paste
>
> If you're working on proprietary code that can't have GNU Public License (GPL) code touching it but there's GPL code that does what you need to do, you may be tempted to copy a few snippets across.
>
> *Don't.*
>
> If there's any contest about your product duplicating GPL code, an audit that diffs your code base against the contested GPL code would quickly reveal your action—putting you and your company in hot water.

Note, however, that the *Lesser* GNU Public License (LGPL) is similar but lessens the restrictions on other code that links to LGPL code. For example, the GNU C Library (glibc) is LGPL, so you can write a program that links to glibc, and it doesn't impose any licensing requirements on your program.

Licenses such as Apache, MIT, and BSD are more permissive. You can usually integrate code using these licenses into your own products without much trouble. The lawyers will still need to approve it, of course, but it's a much easier discussion than GPL.

Now that we have some flags on the legal minefield, let's discuss workflow.

Tracking Upstream Projects

Say you need an XML parser for your company's Ruby-based product, and the built-in one doesn't do the job. You find an open source XML parser, and it looks perfect—even the license.

You happily download the current version (let's say it's 1.0), write your code, and check the whole ball of wax into version control. Great, problem solved...for today. A month later, you run into a bug and discover it's already fixed in the latest version (1.2). So, you download the latest and then discover, oh no, you've customized some things in the old version; just shoving in the new version will wipe out your changes. Now you need to merge.

The problem here is you can only do a *two-way merge*: you have your changed version based on 1.0, plus the new version 1.2. Your merge tool only knows where lines are different—it can't tell where the differences originated from. The burden is entirely on you to figure it out.

Your version control system can help if you use it correctly. For the basics, see Tip 13, *Control Time (and Timelines)*, on page 87. The key for tracking external code is to create a *vendor branch* that always tracks the upstream code exactly as it comes from the open source project.

Figure 6, *Tracking external code with a vendor branch*, on page 97 shows how things should look. Now when you get to merging your changes (1.0a) with the upstream changes (1.2), the version control system can do a *three-way merge* between these two plus their common parents. In many cases, the tool can do a totally hands-off merge, saving you a bunch of time. It's much less error-prone than manual merging, too.

Contributing to Open Source Projects

So far, we've been concerned with pulling in open source components. What about pushing changes back out? Say you find a bug, fix it for your own use, and want to push it back to the community. Sounds like a no-brainer, but your company may treat *all* of your work as proprietary. You'll need to get management's permission first.

Then it's time to prepare your change. The checklist will depend on the project, but assume that you'll need to write a detailed change description, demonstrate its quality based on the project's standards, and ensure the change compiles and runs on other target machines (where applicable).

Then it's time to submit. The mechanics depend on the project, but they usually look like this:

- Generate a patch set and email it to a project mailing list. Use your version control tool to generate the patch. The project maintainers will consider the patch, and if they like it, they'll commit it to the project's repository.

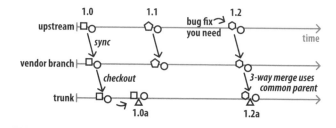

Figure 6—Tracking external code with a vendor branch

Contributing Back: Keep It Pragmatic

Does your manager need some convincing on the value of contributing to open source projects? The best argument isn't a philosophical "it's the right thing to do" speech. Warm fuzzies don't pay the bills.

Instead, keep it pragmatic: if you make changes to a project, you have two options:

- Maintain your changes locally. Every time you pull a new version of code from the community, you'll need to merge in your changes.

- Contribute your changes. No locally maintained patch sets, no merges.

The latter is a win in the long run. Convince management that the changes aren't trade secrets and that it's *less* hassle to contribute them to the community.

- For projects using a hosted version control system (like GitHub[14]), you'll want to fork the project repository, apply your changes, and then generate a *pull request* to the project maintainer. This is a more automated version than emailing patches but accomplishes the same thing.

- You may be granted commit privileges to the project's source code repository, allowing you to submit changes directly. You'll need to establish a solid track record first.

Project maintainers *want* contributions, and they'll encourage and help you get changes in, but they may reject a change

---

14. http://github.com/

you submit. It could be a quality issue—treat this just like a code review in your day job. Or your change may not fit with their long-term plans.

You can choose whether you want to adapt your code to the project's desires or just keep your change in your own repository. Where possible, use this as an opportunity to learn from the project's maintainers. (Also, a record of open source contributions looks great on your resume.)

When you get a change into a project, you may get bug reports. You'll need to investigate them and submit fixes, again just like your day job. On the plus side, that's a bug your company could have hit, too.

Actions

Pick an open source project of your liking, and then do the following:

- Find its license and answer the questions from *Licenses*, on page 94.

- Make your own copy of the project in a way that you can track updates and also maintain your own changes. With GitHub, this is as simple as cloning and creating your own branch—so give that a shot. Other projects may require a bit more work to create the vendor branch and sync upstream changes.

- Investigate the process for submitting a change to the project. (Bonus points: look at the project's bug list, fix one, and submit it.)

Part II

People Skills

CHAPTER 3

Manage Thy Self

Throughout your career you'll have a number of managers. The manager who has the most vested interest in your success over the long haul is *you*.

You get only a partial say in your management, of course—the company-appointed manager will have their own opinions. Your manager might be a great person, actively working to help you succeed and grow in your career. Let's at least assume your manager is not evil. Most likely, he's busy and would *like* to help you succeed, but most of the time he's swamped by an ever-present backlog of meetings and email.

That's why the responsibility ultimately lies with you. You don't have to do everything solo—try to get regular one-on-one time with your manager, and don't be shy about asking for advice—but don't ever let your career and happiness slide because someone else didn't take charge.

- We start by formalizing another source of advice. Tip 15, *Find a Mentor*, on page 103 gives you a reliable person to ask about matters of code and company politics.

- Next, dress codes may not apply to programmers, but in Tip 16, *Own the Image You Project*, on page 107 we discuss how your self-presentation matters a lot more than you may think.

- Next we step back to image as it's projected over time: Tip 17, *Be Visible*, on page 110 deals with how you'll want to project your image within the company.

- About a year into your career, you'll get *very* interested in how your manager perceives you. Tip 18, *Ace Your Performance Review*, on page 114 helps you through the annual performance review.

- Your first years should be filled with vigor and enthusiasm. When that wears down, Tip 19, *Manage Your Stress*, on page 121 coaches you toward sustainable health.

- Finally, Tip 20, *Treat Your Body Right*, on page 127 gives practical advice on ergonomics—and gives you an excuse to go shopping.

Tip 15

Find a Mentor

 [*White Belt*] Your mentor can help you from day one and ideally for years to come.

Where this book is a virtual guide, the most successful programmers will have a real-life guide for the journey, too. Such a guide—or *mentor*—will provide wisdom and council for *you personally* on your first programming job.

The mentor's role is to do the following:

- Help you when you get stuck on the job. They've been programming long enough to have great problem-solving and debugging chops, so even when they don't know all the answers, they can point out the next steps you should take.

- Model behaviors and skills you want to learn. Time spent watching over their shoulder will inspire you to learn new programming tricks and new ways of thinking about your problem domain.

- Keep your career pointed in the right direction. They know how to get ahead in your company and can advise you when opportunities to advance come up.

- Likewise, keep you from shooting yourself in the foot. They'll warn you of hazards specific to your company, like the people you don't want to make enemies with or programming screw-ups that will especially irk your manager. Your mentor has been around long enough to know the turf.

This mentor may be one person, or it could be several—for example, you might tag along with a senior programmer on your team but learn the political lay of the land from your manager. I'll speak of a singular mentor in this tip. The same advice, however, applies to more than one.

Qualities of a Great Mentor

Before we get into finding the mentor, let's consider the qualities of the person you want to find.

On Your Side

First and foremost, a great mentor is interested in your personal growth. This person needs to be on *your side* and will always push for your success. Some companies have policies that put peers in contest with each other; your mentor, however, must be someone who has nothing to lose from your success.

Technical Skill

Obviously, a great mentor for a programmer should be a great programmer. Let's distill that a little further: you're looking for someone who has domain expertise for the product you're working on, has a track record of delivering solid code, and otherwise demonstrates the skills you want to attain.

Under the umbrella of "programming" there are a zillion subdomains of specialized knowledge. If you're working on a large-scale website, for example, there's a whole career's worth of skills you could learn about scalable server-side programming. You'll want a mentor who has *domain expertise* in this area.

The track record is equally important. There are genius programmers who have rocket-science raw talent but just can't focus and get a product out the door. Industry is pragmatic; you need to write solid code *and* you need to ship the product. Look for a mentor who's demonstrated skill at both.

Looking for skill comes with a qualification: great programmers are not necessarily great teachers. Perhaps they can't explain how they work because they're guided by intuition more than a process. Or perhaps they simply don't have the patience to work with junior programmers. Make sure your mentor is someone you can actually learn from.

Knows the Lay of the Land

A key role of your mentor is passing on *tribal knowledge*—all the undocumented stuff that gets passed on person to person within the company. You've probably heard about specifications, style guides, wikis, and other documents that are supposed to help programmers get up to speed. Nobody wants to admit it, but *they're all out-of-date.* You'll need someone who's been working on the product for a while to show you around.

A great mentor has been with the organization long enough to know the politics and has earned respect both within the team and within the company. As we'll discuss in Tip 22, *Connect the Dots*, on page 141, it takes a while to discover who's pals with whom, but your mentor can give you a big head start. Further, your mentor can warn you of political strife that's best to stay away from.

High Standards

To grow in skill, you need someone to hold you to a higher standard than you're currently at. A great mentor will help you first meet the needs of the product—which, in turn, keeps your paycheck coming—but also tell you where you can improve.

It takes some humility on your part to accept this above-and-beyond guidance, but remember, the guidance of your mentor isn't just for getting the job done today; it's also for growing into a senior programmer later.

If you're looking for someone who will hold you to high standards, look for people who hold *themselves* to high standards. Who has a lot of books on their shelves? Who has a reputation for discovering new technologies and programming practices?

Find Your Mentor

Now for finding your mentor. First, ask your manager. You don't need to get fancy; start with, "Who should I ask for help if I get stuck?" Or more formally, "Is there someone on the team who could mentor me as I get started?" A manager will often have a mentor in mind.

Second, consult your peers. When taking a task in a planning meeting, ask, "If I need help on this task, can someone lend me a hand?" Or ask of a senior peer, "You seem to know a lot about [this domain], so can you give me any pointers before I start on this task?"

Not all mentoring relationships are of the formal, long-term variety. If your manager assigns a mentor, by all means take it. But even in a casual environment you can find informal, short-term mentoring to help you with a programming task. Those informal mentors could be all of your peers on the team, at various times.

If you're not given a long-term mentor, try to find one on your own. You'll want the big-picture guidance and encouragement. Ask of someone who you'd like to mentor you, for example, "I really appreciate the help you've been giving me. Would you consider mentoring me on an ongoing basis?" The key word *mentoring* is the cue that you're seeking big-picture advice, not just help for hitting the next deadline.

Mentor vs. Manager

Some questions are more appropriate for your manager than a mentor. When you need assistance in a more official variety, for example related to your benefits or pay, that's the domain of your manager. If there's business-related issues like a failed production system or you've discovered a critical bug, your manager needs to know.

Your manager can provide a lot of mentoring, too. A good manager will be looking out for everyone on their team already, trying to eliminate short-term obstacles and helping with long-term career goals. However, a manager also has obligations to the business that can interfere with mentoring. For example, if your manager is tasked with laying off 20 percent of the team, your manager is no longer an objective source of advice on career planning.

Actions

Your first action should be clear: *find a mentor*! Start informally if you must. Try not to go longer than a year without a more formal mentor.

Tip 16

Own the Image You Project

 [*White Belt*] First impressions matter. Think about this topic before your first day on the job.

First, a disclaimer: there are "corporate image consultants" who specialize in helping people dress for success. I'm not one of them.

Programmers may not be judged by their clothes as much as, say, executives or salespeople. Even so, the people around us have their biases. You can choose to challenge them or decide you're better off picking a different battle. Either way, *choose consciously*.

Perceptions

We humans haven't lost our capacity for instinct — we will make snap decisions about situations and people in a split second. The R-mode, pattern-matching part of our brain will make a decision before any conscious thought has time to process. "That person looks scary" or "That person looks professional" are thoughts that will run through our mind before the person has time to say a word.

This value judgment may be right or may be wrong. Malcolm Gladwell, in his book *Blink* [Gla06], describes this judgment as a necessary way of dealing with the many people around us. We simply can't afford the time to get to know everyone we meet on a deep, personal level before making any judgment about them. However, we have a skill of forming first impressions that serves us surprisingly well. It's not perfect, but it has a darn good hit rate for taking only a couple seconds.

Look at how you're dressed right now in the mirror. What value judgment would a stranger make in the first two seconds of meeting you? (Aside from *shockingly attractive,* of course.) Is that the image you *want* to project?

Norms

Our perceptions are shaped by our environment; what is "normal" for the region, industry, and company we occupy? A design firm in San Francisco is a fundamentally different environment—nearly a different universe—than a banking firm in New York City.

There are times it pays to stick with the norm. Your first couple weeks on the job is not the best time to make a bold statement. Meeting with a customer (when those opportunities come up) is a good time to look professional. These are times when you need to make good first impressions and/or represent your company well.

You can challenge the norms once you've earned some credibility on your team. For most West Coast companies, anything goes. (In East Coast and international settings, ask and look around.) Programmers have more freedom than most. At least in places I've worked, dying your hair purple and wearing knee-high boots (regardless of your gender) would hardly get a second look.

Of course, you may choose to stick with the norm on clothing and be bold in other ways; you could be the woman who gives Takahashi Method presentations with huge, bold text. Or you could be the guy who writes meeting agendas in Haiku.

Own Your Style

Whichever direction you choose for personal style, *own it*. You need to be confident in the image you project. If you can't look in the mirror and think to yourself, "That's me," then fix it.

An example from my own life: I took the advice of "dress like the person whose job you want" and bought several traditional, corporate-style patterned shirts. After a couple months I stopped wearing them because I felt like a phony in corporate blue with pinstripes, and I'm sure that showed in my body language.

If you make a change, "try on" your new style starting on a Saturday. That gives you a few days out of the office to get used to it. Monday might shock some of your co-workers, but the key is it won't shock *you*. I learned this tip after shaving my head on a Tuesday. Mistake. Not only did my co-workers hardly recognize me the next morning, I hardly recognized myself.

Neatness Counts

No matter what your style, do it *with style*. No matter if it's jeans, dress, or slacks, keep them clean. Long hair or bald, get a trim now and then. People make a subconscious link between the neatness in your grooming and the neatness of your work.

Furthermore, *you* make a mental shift when you put some care into getting ready for work in the morning. If you roll out of bed and stumble into the office disheveled and half asleep, your work will reflect that. If you prepare thoughtfully for the day, your work will reflect *that*.

Actions

- Take a half hour—enough time to think about this for real—and write down a description of the image you want to project at work. If that's not the image you're projecting now, what do you need to change?

- Pull all the clothes out of your closet. Only put back the pieces that are still your style and fit well. Donate or sell the rest.

Tip 17

Be Visible

 [*Brown Belt*]   You need to start with simply doing your job well. Then you move onto getting noticed for it.

Whatever role you have, you need to establish a positive reputation. That reputation magnifies the *visibility* of your role. Visibility is when people around the office know your name—"I've heard of Emma; she does awesome work." Not only does it stroke your ego, but it gives you influence to get the projects and roles you want down the road.

Visibility doesn't require a fancy job title; it's far more subtle. You, as a lowly programmer on the bottom of the org chart, can have visibility all the way up to the CEO. If you're working on a project the CEO has personal interest in, you have visibility. You could have stumbled into it by accident; this happened to me when I overhauled the user interface graphics for a product I was working on. The graphics were simply a hobby, not really part of my job, but the CEO *loved* the new look, and I was *in*.

You don't always get visibility by accident, yet pushing for visibility can backfire. It's something of a zen thing—people who overtly seek it come off looking like phonies. You know that guy in meetings who's always piping up just so he gets a word in and sounds smart, but really he sounds like a meathead instead? Don't be that guy.

The better approach is to let your work do the talking. First, while you're new in your programming job, strive to get some early wins. If you have any say in the matter, take on some tasks that you *know* you can deliver quickly and solidly. Follow the company coding style perfectly, write unit tests that prove functionality, and make it *really* good and deliver fast.

Don't Use Duct Tape, Velcro Looks Better

The year was 1996, well before cell phones did anything more than make phone calls, and a company called Metricom was selling a radio modem with inexpensive data service. I bought one and started poking at it; it turns out its serial interface was dead simple.

I was working on the networking stack for our company's handheld computer. It had a phone jack on it for connecting to a dial-up ISP. (Back then, dial-up was the norm.) I looked at our computer, looked at the radio modem, and it was blindingly obvious that these two were made for each other. So, I got some Velcro and stuck the two together.

It didn't take long to attract attention. *Everyone* in the company wanted to check it out. At a conference a couple months later I wrote a small web server application and passed it around —people could edit a web page on-screen, and others could browse to it in real time. It was a hit.

If there's one thing geeks can't resist, it's plugging stuff together. In this case, our handheld computer just *begged* to be untethered from the phone line, so even nongeeks could appreciate the coolness of this combo. I was still a lowly programmer, but everyone in the company knew my name from then on.

Your manager will notice, and he'll go bragging to *his* manager about making a good hire. "Our new programmer Emma has been here only a month, and her code went into test with zero defects. Clearly I'm a genius for hiring her." (OK, that's a little bit of an exaggeration, but only a little.)

Second, make a mark on the product where others will notice. Let's say you get stuck on bug patrol—a common new-hire task, purportedly to help you "learn the code base," but really it's because the other programmers just don't want to fix the bugs themselves. Your first task is to fix some GUI text fields that don't validate correctly. Do that and check it in, and then go through and make sure the GUI widgets line up right—do some visual housekeeping that makes the interface look nicer than you found it. "Emma went through and polished this part of the GUI, and *wow*, it looks a lot better!"

Finally, as you get more credibility in the group and freedom to pick your tasks, pick some things that people in the

Industry Perspective: Making an Impression

The most important thing you as a new/freshman programmer can do is keep your head down and be *certain* you're doing the task at hand. Any opinion, idea, or suggestion you may have regarding the workflow of the company, or the product you are on, should be withheld at least until after the first review cycle.

Any person straight out of school wants to make a big impression; you want to show the company that you're worth your salt and said company is full of geniuses for hiring you. And that's great. The problem is that trying to make this impression can throw you into over-reaction mode, especially if you have a highly competitive personality.

New employees can (and do) have great, fresh ideas. The problem is you don't know where the corporate land mines are, you don't yet have awareness of what factions are competing within the corporate climate, and you don't have a good enough feel for the corporate culture.

Putting it another way, what gets you a raise and kudos at Google may well get you fired at Netflix.

Nothing, and I mean *nothing*, speaks louder than doing the job you're assigned to the absolute best you possibly can.

—*Mark "The Red" Harlan, engineering manager*

company are passionate about. It could be as simple as tying a couple features together in a novel way, like adding an email gateway to a web application. "Emma made it so I can email an update to the tracking system without having to log in—what a great idea!" There's always *some* itch that people have wanted to scratch but haven't put in the effort.

Visibility may sound like shameless self-promotion. Yes, to a degree it is. But when the next job opening comes up or the next cool project is getting started, don't you want a shot? If your name has been circulating among the managers because of something cool you did, you're much more likely to get that shot.

And let's be honest, programmers love to build cool stuff. When you've built something cool, it's really fun to show it off. So, *show it off* and enjoy your moment in the spotlight.

Actions

Consider the work you have on your plate. Are there opportunities for early wins? Grab some tasks and truly nail them.

Looking ahead, can you make a dent in your product in a way that others will notice? It may be a shiny new feature, but it could also be fixing an annoying bug, too.

Tip 18

Ace Your Performance Review

 [*White Belt*]   Your performance review isn't for a year, but start logging your accomplishments early.

Consider the poor, hapless software manager: once a year she has to write reviews for all her employees and try to state, in objective and quantifiable terms, how they did on a job that's intrinsically abstract.

Attempts to quantify programmer performance have never gone well. For example, the junior manager might try to measure *how much* code a programmer writes. During Apple's get-it-done push to ship the Lisa computer, managers decided to track the lines of code written each week by each programmer. Bill Atkinson reworked a good amount of the graphics code, making it simpler and much faster —and also shorter. He logged negative 2,000 lines of code for the week.[1] What does a manager do with *that?*

Of course, that's your manager's problem—*mostly.* It becomes your problem when it's your performance they're trying to measure and your paycheck that's affected.

When it's time to review your performance for the year, you have one essential goal: *you need to give your manager the best information possible so you get the best review possible.* This has nothing to do with greed; it's simply making sure she's aware of your accomplishments for the year. You've worked hard, so get credit for it.

Performance Review Mechanics

Companies do performance reviews for obvious reasons: they want to identify who's doing great and who isn't. They

---

1.   http://folklore.org/StoryView.py?story=Negative_2000_Lines_Of_Code.txt

Industry Perspective: Performance Review Prep

Do your homework ahead of time. Learn what's in the review process and especially who is expected to contribute to your review. Take a look at a blank review form to see the kinds of things you'll be graded on.

About a month ahead of time, informally poll all the people you know who will be included in the process (including your boss) and say, "Hey, man, my review is coming up; how does it seem like I'm doing?" Do this in person, not by email. Make it seem easy and offhanded—not serious like a heart attack. Be sure to work on anything you hear that's negative.

If your company has them, write your self-review with the formal review in mind. Be sure to focus on numbers and productivity (for example, "My applet makes the new build system go two times faster"), but never exaggerate.

All companies care about timeliness and quality as well as your ability to work both individually and as a team. Cover all those bases.

Think about the way your boss sees your job. If there's something she doesn't know about that's important in what you do, be sure to mention it in detail.

—*Mark "The Red" Harlan, engineering manager*

want to reward the great, and…we'll get to the other side later.

Raises in salary are usually tied to the performance review, and the raise budget is usually a fixed amount for the whole department. Assuming it's been a good year for the business, the department is allocated a budget for raises. Let's say it allows for a 3 percent overall raise. They could just give 3 percent to everybody and be done. Often, however, they want to give more to the stars (like 5 percent) and less to the slackers (like nothing).

Thus, we get back to the hapless manager: she has to document who are the stars and who are the slackers. Let's look at common approaches used to create this document.

The Self-Review

The first approach is to punt the review to *you*. You get a form that says, in formalish terms, "What have you done for the company lately?" Take this review very seriously: there's a good chance that much of its content will be copied and pasted into your official review.

As you go through the year, you need to be collecting material for the self-review. There are five major buckets to fill.

Quality

Here we want anything that can show you're writing solid code: defect rate per line of code, bugs fixed, test cases written, and such. They don't need to be hard measures: positive comments from co-workers, design principles you started applying, or improvements you've made to your team's test infrastructure are all helpful.

Examples: "Fixed forty-two product defects, including five severity-one defects." "Consistently unit-tested code, with 2:1 average test case to application code ratio."

Quantity

Fortunately, quantities are easier to measure: features completed, product releases shipped, source code commits, and so forth, are good fodder. Don't forget the version control system; it can give you lots of statistics about what you've changed in the code base.

Also, keep in mind that code is only part of your job. Anything that benefits the business is worth considering

Examples: "Shipped version 1.2 of Widget Factory in my role as a widget programmer." "Assisted customer support, providing key information to resolve four support tickets."

Timeliness

You don't get assignments without an expectation of when you'll get it finished. Track your hit rate and—assuming it's not terrible—report it in your self-review. This is much easier in agile environments where you review progress every couple weeks.

Examples: "Delivered on project commitments with 82 percent success rate." "Completed tasks within 70 percent of original estimates."

Cost Savings to Company

Programmers have a reputation for driving costs *up* rather than down. However, managers are always looking for ways to stretch their budgets, so if you have something to brag about here, brag.

Examples: "Improved message handling capability from 100 emails/second to 150 emails/second, thus making better use of company servers." "Compressed data in less-used database columns, reducing storage footprint by 42 percent with negligible impact to performance."

Making the Team Look Good

Your team's value within the company isn't just an equation like revenue contribution vs. cost. Perception counts just as much as any numbers. Any kudos you bring in for the team—and therefore your manager—are worth mentioning.

Examples: "Analyzed web server logs and identified top bounce pages; improved these pages and increased visitor retention." "Improved GUI look-and-feel before important trade show, earning positive comments from company representatives at the show."

Finally, one note about what *not* to include: don't clutter the self-review with tasks that are considered business overhead. "Attended 942 meetings" can be left off.

When you get the self-review form, ask your manager how much detail to include. If you've been good about logging accomplishments over the year, you'll have more than enough content, so pick the best. If not, jog your memory by reviewing old email or scanning your commits in the version control system.

The 360-Degree Review

The next review-writing approach is to punt the problem to your peers. The manager picks a couple other programmers and a couple people from other parts of the company that have worked with you over the year.

Your manager may ask you for candidate reviewers. Who in the company has the best impression of your work? You need to know, well ahead of time, who your allies are across the company.

Here's where it pays to wander beyond the bounds of the engineering cubes, as discussed in Tip 26, *Know Your (Corporate) Anatomy*, on page 163. If you can reply to your manager with 360 reviewers that include your product's support lead and product manager, for example, you're well on your way to an awesome review.

The Manager's Review

Finally, having as much of the review written by other people as possible, it's the manager's turn to craft the final review. It may be—like many reviews I received—your self-review with some annotations by the manager and a few comments from the 360 reviews tacked onto the end. Your manager isn't getting paid to compose great literature here.

The review from your manager shouldn't come as a surprise. Any reasonable manager will be giving you kudos and tips for improvement throughout the year. The document you get handed should be a summary of those.

Ranking

Many larger companies require managers to rank their employees. It's the same thing as grading on a curve: the human resources department asserts that each team's performance follows a normal distribution with a couple rock stars, a couple slackers, and a bunch of normal folks in the middle.

This will show up as something like a one to four rank indicating which quartile you're in. If you're in the not-so-great bucket, see *Performance Improvement*, on page 119. Otherwise, don't worry about it.

Here's a dirty secret: *every manager loathes ranking employees.* The manager puts a ton of effort into hiring an awesome team, and then HR comes along and asserts that the team must have a certain number of slackers.

Promotion

Some teams have designated technical leads or other promotion roles where you still program for your day job. Your

Performance Improvement

There may come a day when you're told you need to improve. If you receive anything written, for example a "performance improvement plan," that's a warning shot that your job is on the line. When it hits writing—email counts—that's management's way of creating the paper trail they need to fire somebody.

I assume you're not slacking. Therefore, there must be a disconnect between what you're doing and what the company needs you to do. The first step is identifying this disconnect in a way that's absolutely clear to both you and your manager. The performance improvement document is a good place to start; this should spell out specific areas that need improvement and specific measures of what that looks like.

Let's say you rolled out buggy code to production. Everyone lets a bug loose once in a while—but you had too many bugs in too short a while. Together with your manager, come up with a plan to make absolutely sure that the quality of your code doesn't come to further question. Examples: line-by-line peer review before committing code, unit tests with 100 percent coverage and peer review of boundary conditions, code inspection with static analysis tools.

Then, relentlessly update your manager on progress. Send a weekly email with progress on each issue identified in the performance improvement plan. Your manager needs to know that you take the problems seriously and that addressing them is your top priority.

recent performance reviews will absolutely factor into discussions of promotion.

There's one additional factor you can influence: you need to act the role before you can get it. For a tech lead, that means a wide breadth of knowledge, sound design decisions, helping others get the project to its next milestone, and the like.

When your manager is looking for a tech lead, she's going to gravitate to the programmer she can most easily visualize in that role. If you're already serving in a fashion that's similar to a tech lead, guess who goes to the front of the list?

Actions

- Create a file, paper or electronic, where you can keep a log of accomplishments for your next performance review. Finish something on time? Make a note and file it. Solve a gnarly bug? File it. Mine this file when it's time to write your self-review.

- As review time approaches, consider who you'd want to give you 360 reviews, and have those ready if asked. Pick two people from your team, two from other departments. Don't just pick friends—pick people who you've done meaningful work with.

- About a month ahead of your review, ask your manager directly, "Since my review is coming up, how am I doing? Is there anything I can improve between now and then?"

Tip 19

Manage Your Stress

 [*Brown Belt*] Let's hope you have some time before you need to stress about this topic.

You love programming, and you love your job. Most of the time you should be having fun. Every job has its ups and downs, however, and it's important for your long-term health to weather the storms gracefully.

Zen teachings have the concept of *mushin no shin*, sometimes translated as "mind like water," wherein you respond to stimuli from your environment in exact proportion to each stimulus. To a martial artist, she would block or strike her opponent with exactly the right amount of force to accomplish the job—neither too little (thus allowing defeat) nor too much (thus succumbing to anger or zeal).

In your own work, the *mushin* mind-set means acting and reacting to the pressures of the job with neither defeat nor anger but instead as a consummate professional.

Of course, this is easier said than done. Even the *mushin* professional who keeps her cool on the job can carry a subconscious burden. You need to recognize the burdens you carry and deal with them in a constructive manner.

Recognizing Stress

Stress reactions may manifest themselves in physical ways: grinding your teeth, tension headaches, or clenched shoulder muscles, for example. While in a place you can relax, take a mental inventory of your body and try to sense muscle tension. Open your jaw wide, and let it come back relaxed. Roll your head gently. Bring your shoulders down. Check in with your body a couple times a day, and over time you'll notice where you tend to carry tension.

Biofeedback

If I told you I could teach you to regulate your heart rate, change the temperature of your skin, or beat a lie detector test, would you believe me?

In biofeedback training, a therapist hooks you up to a bunch of sensors like muscle activation (EMG), skin conductance, skin temperature, exhaled CO2 pressure, and so forth. You're measuring properties of your autonomic nervous system (ANS), which are things you can't consciously sense and control.

With the real-time feedback provided by the instrumentation, you *can* learn to sense what your ANS is doing. For example, if you carry tension in your shoulders, an EMG probe can show you exactly what's going on there, even if you can't feel it. With training, you can both learn to feel — and then control — problem areas in your body.

(As an added bonus, a polygraph test also measures autonomic nervous system responses. You get where I'm going.)

If you're struggling with stress, see whether there's a biofeedback therapist in your area. If nothing else, try a couple sessions just because it's truly fascinating. One last tip — don't be afraid if you notice the therapist is a *psychiatrist* instead of a *doctor*. They're usually shrinks. Don't stress over it.

Observe your interactions with other people: are you quick to anger with co-workers when you're normally mellow? Are others angry with you? Maybe you notice yourself skipping lunch when you used to hang with friends. Or during team meetings you're usually the optimist in the room, but lately you've taken on a tone of defeat.

Finally, observe patterns of your day that may have changed. Most of us are creatures of habit — coffee in the morning, walking to lunch, checking a couple blogs in the afternoon, playing a favorite computer game. Have these changed recently?

This kind of introspection takes a certain self-honesty that may feel uncomfortable (or just goofy) at first. It's a valid feeling, and since you're being honest with yourself, go ahead and acknowledge it. Then let it go.

Addressing Physical Stress

The physical component of stress is a symptom of psychological stress, but when it becomes a problem in itself, it feeds back and creates *more* stress. There are a number of ways to break the cycle:

- Massage therapy can be very therapeutic and have long-lasting effects, depending on the practitioner and your body's response.

- Biofeedback techniques (see *Biofeedback,* on page 122) can teach you to both recognize and release tension.

- Exercise can exhaust muscles and release tension—plus give your mind a break from the computer. (Many tech companies have gyms or provide discounted gym memberships.)

- Fix any ergonomic problems with your workstation, as discussed in Tip 20, *Treat Your Body Right*, on page 127.

You'll need to find what works for you, of course. But do find something—your physical stress won't go away on its own.

Long Hours

When you work a salaried job, you are required to get the job done, regardless of how many hours it takes. *Reasonable* managers will work with you to match your duties to a roughly forty-hour week. Some insist on specific hours (aka butt-in-chair time); others don't care.

I've worked in start-ups that mandated sixty-hour minimum work weeks. That's part of the gig with start-ups—whether they say it explicitly or not, be prepared for it.

When you're young, single, and love your job, long hours aren't a problem. I worked like crazy the first several years of my career and had a great time doing it. If this is where you're at, go nuts; that's what the energy of youth is for!

Also, accept that, as a newbie, it's going to take you longer to get the job done than an experienced programmer. You'll go down more dead-end paths, make more mistakes, and struggle more with debugging. That's part of the learning experience, and it takes time.

Later you'll pick up responsibilities outside of work—spouse, kids, a house to maintain—and those long hours become a real problem. You have several options to consider:

- Optimize your butt-in-chair time. Look at techniques like Pomodoro[2] and GTD[3] to focus your time in the office so you can leave earlier.

- Bring in lunch from home instead of going out. You can eat at your desk in ten minutes; going out often takes an hour. (However, *do* go out with your co-workers from time to time just to shoot the breeze.)

- Take your crunch times in smaller, more frequent doses. If you have project milestones every week or two, then you may need to dedicate only a day every couple weeks for crunch time. By contrast, when milestones are every six months, that's a lot of time for a project to get off-track, and crunch times can last for weeks (or months).

- Find a company whose culture values work-life balance. This doesn't necessarily mean big, slow-moving companies with nine-to-five cultures; there are plenty of small companies whose founders burned out on killer hours themselves.

You can get a lot done in a focused forty hours. The young bucks spending their lives at the office aren't always that productive—the office becomes a place of socialization and recreation in addition to work; it's not sixty straight hours of coding.

Burnout

In cycling there's a state of fatigue known as *the bonk*. Your body uses glycogen to keep the muscles going, but after hours of pedaling, it runs out. When that happens, the bonk comes on suddenly, and you want to fall off the bike and pass out.

---

2. *Pomodoro Technique Illustrated* [Nö09]
3. *Getting Things Done: The Art of Stress-Free Productivity* [All02]

Burning out in your job feels much the same. All the sudden you have an extreme compulsion to quit your job and become a Tibetan yak herder. Or dig ditches. It doesn't really matter—just *anything* except typing another line of code.

It's usually not the code that causes burnout. More often it's mismanagement: mandatory long hours, death march scheduling, and the like. I'm sure you can stand occasional periods of high stress, but when those periods stretch over months or years, you *will* burn out.

In cycling you can avoid the bonk by eating simple carbs as you ride. Likewise, you can avoid burnout by getting away from the code and having some fun. (This is why so many high-tech companies have foosball tables.) However, carbs and fun only delay the inevitable: at some point you need to take a *real* break and rest. I don't mean a long weekend, either: if you've been scrambling for months to ship version 1.0, you'll need weeks (or more) of vacation to let yourself recover.

If you don't allow recovery time and you drive yourself to burnout—you'll know when you do—take some comfort that it doesn't last forever. You may need to herd yaks for a year, but you'll get the itch to start programming again.

Take a Vacation

Programmers—especially of the unmarried variety—are terrible about taking vacations. It seems like you're always in the middle of a big project and you'd get behind if you took a week off. Face it, *there's never a good time* to take vacation. Just go.

Don't limit yourself to the "obligatory vacations" where you visit family on holidays. Go do something interesting. Try windsurfing, rock climbing, scuba diving, going overseas…anything to get your head out of computers for a while. Try the Geek Atlas[4] if you're struggling for ideas. As you get older, these opportunities are harder to come by, so get going now.

---

4.   http://www.geekatlas.com

Why bother? Why spend the time and money? Vacations are where you reset your perspective. You can't tell you're in a rut while you're in it—you need to see it from an outside vantage point. Further, it's a lot easier to stave off burnout *before* you burn out.

Take It Seriously

Stress can be a good thing for motivating positive change in your life. It can also be incredibly destructive. Depression, like burnout, sends you into a downward spiral that's extremely difficult to break out of.

If you've been heading downward for a while, get help from trusted friends or a professional. Don't be embarrassed or pretend it's not a problem—you'll pull out a lot faster with help.

Actions

- Try to recognize your body's physical stress responses. If it's something you can directly control (like muscle tension), then get in the habit of recognizing it and letting it go. If it's an autonomic response (such as increased heart rate or panic attack), then work with a biofeedback therapist.

- Try this experiment: next week, when you hit forty hours of office time, go home. Don't return until next Monday. Depending on your company's culture, you may not be able to pull this off regularly, but make it a goal.

Tip 20

Treat Your Body Right

 [*Brown Belt*] You don't need to optimize ergonomics on day one, at least if you're young. However, don't put it off more than a year or two.

How is it that so many people get injured sitting behind a desk? It's not like you pull a muscle when trying to lift an especially heavy line of code or bloody your forehead by whacking into a nasty program fault. Instead, physical injury for programmers is the sum of zillions of small things compounded over time—more akin to being pecked to death by ducks than going out in a bang.

Repetitive strain and stress-related problems are solvable. Like most problems, they're best solved before they become a problem. A little bit of attention to the issues *now* could save you considerable trouble later.

Workstation Makeover

Computers are marketed on speed, memory, and sometimes disk space. Never does a manufacturer tout its keyboard. Yet you're a lot better off with a junker CPU and putting money into a keyboard that fits your hand, a display mounted at eye level, and a mouse that tracks well.

Choosing a Keyboard

Keyboards are notorious for their badness. Their arrangement of keys has hardly changed since the days of mechanical typebars. Key travel, the distance a key moves from its up to down position, is often minimal and mushy. Worse, so-called natural shapes often make even less sense than their normal counterparts. Don't put up with it; buy something that fits you. Usually the company will reimburse you, but use your own cash if they won't.

Here are a few things to look for in a good keyboard:

- Appropriate travel and feel. Length of travel is a matter of personal preference. Most people prefer a solid, tactile click at the bottom and quick rebound. Try the keyboard in a store if you can.

- Key positioning that makes sense. Oddly, the vast majority of keyboards have diagonal columns—you need to look hard for keyboards that break from the norm. True vertical rows match the flex of your fingers much more naturally. Also, programmers use modifier keys much more than most people, so keyboards with modifier keys in the bottom corners do us a great disservice.

- Key bed that fits your hand. Hold your hand palm-down and flex your fingers through their range of motion. If you imagined a keyboard there, its keys would be in the shape of a cup, right? Avoid "natural" keyboards that have the opposite shape; they make you reach *further* for the outer rows than a flat keyboard.

The only keyboard I've found that truly matches the hand is the Kinesis Contoured. It's expensive and mail-order only. I also like the action on certain generations of Apple keyboards, even if their key arrangement is traditional. Others swear by older generations of IBM keyboard. You'll probably need to try a few and find what you like.

Don't worry about connectors (PS/2, USB, and so on); find what matches *you* and buy an adapter to match your computer.

Display

We've seen a "two steps forward, one step back" trend in displays. We've taken several steps forward in terms of LCD technology, size, brightness, and contrast. We've taken a few steps back in terms of resolution and screen finish.

At least one study has correlated increased display resolution with increased productivity. It's easy to imagine programming scenarios where it's helpful to see code, a debugger, and your application all at once. However, there are plenty of scenarios where it's helpful to focus on *one* thing at a time. Go high-res for the times you need it; hide background applications when you need to focus.

Note that *high-resolution* and *big* are two different measures. You might be tempted to buy an HDTV, but keep in mind that a 20-inch 1080p display and a 40-inch 1080p display have *exactly the same* number of pixels. Bigger pixels don't buy you much unless your eyes are bad.

Look for an antiglare screen coating. Don't be fooled by glossy coatings; they're a cheap trick to boost the perceived contrast of the display. They act like a mirror for glare (and everything else).

Finally, don't look down at the monitor; mount it high enough that you can look straight ahead at it. This might require fiddling with your furniture or buying a mounting arm.

Desk Rodent

Most people use a mouse or trackpad for cursor movement. With good text editing habits, you won't need it much during programming; see *Text Editor*, on page 61 for more details. Mice and graphics tablets are preferable at the desktop because you can use larger muscle groups to move them.

Scroll wheels on mice, unlike the mouse itself, require fine muscle movement. Dinky scroll wheels aren't worth using; some mice have large, free-spinning scroll wheels that are vastly superior. Other convenience factors like wireless connections and optical tracking are tremendously nice. Long gone are the days of tangled mouse cables and lint on the wheels. If you're still putting up with either, upgrade.

If you notice wrist, arm, or shoulder pain on only one side of your body, the mouse may be the culprit. Try switching your mouse to the other hand. You can also set up your office and home workstations with the mouse on opposite sides. (There's no need to buy a left-handed mouse; it's not hard to use a righty mouse with your left hand.)

Desk and Chair

You don't have to find a super-fancy chair; you just need to find a chair that fits you. The Herman Miller Aeron chair is legendary as the ultimate in fancy ergonomic chairs. However, it doesn't fit me, and it may not fit you, either. I discovered my perfect chair (the Herman Miller Equa) in

Measuring Muscle Activation

If you want to get *really* nerdy about ergonomics, find a biofeedback or physical therapist with a surface electromyograph (SEMG). It's a machine that measures electrical impulses in your muscles, and it can detect muscle activation that's far too subtle for you to perceive.

With sensors on your trapezius muscles, for example, the SEMG can tell you whether your keyboard and chair positions are correct for allowing those muscles to relax. Minor changes in position make the difference between your traps idling at a couple millivolts or spasming at tens of millivolts. You won't notice it while you're sitting there—but over the course of many days at your desk, that muscle activation can lead to pain and tension headache.

Nerdy? Absolutely. But a couple sessions of in-office biofeedback training will pay you back for decades to come.

the conference rooms at a previous company. It's utilitarian and absolutely not a status symbol, but it *fits me*.

Some people use exercise balls at their desk, kneeling chairs, and other oddities. These are fine as long as you can maintain a proper curve in your back. You may not know what "proper" feels like, but a doctor or chiropractor can help.

Finally, no matter how good your chair, the human body isn't built to sit at a desk all day long. Consider standing. Cubicles are easy to modify; raise your work surface height and give it a shot.

Optimize Yourself

Most guides to ergonomics focus entirely on your workstation and ignore the other component of the equation: *you*. It's worth the time and expense to optimize your workstation for minimum strain, but it's equally worthwhile to optimize your own body for the tasks you need it to perform.

Efficiency

The single best skill you can learn is proper touch-typing. I know it sounds silly. *Of course* you can type; you're a programmer. But do you *really* type well? I found out the hard way, when I switched to a Kinesis keyboard, that I didn't actually type correctly—my left hand was shifted over a column, and I never used my pinkie fingers. My accuracy and speed increased considerably after retraining.

There's no secret to touch-typing; it's more an exercise in discipline (and, initially, frustration). One trick to keep you honest: paint the keys on your keyboard. I painted mine all different colors. It draws some attention in the office.

Some people also use alternative keyboard layouts; the usual QWERTY keyboard isn't the only game in town. The Dvorak layout, in particular, is designed to minimize finger travel for English text. You can switch most any computer to Dvorak just by looking in the keyboard layouts, usually in system preferences under International keyboard support.

I use the Dvorak layout, and it delivers on its promise to reduce finger travel and therefore to make typing more comfortable in the long-run. The switch, however, was *very* difficult. It took about two months to get my typing speed back. Consider Dvorak if you need to use a laptop full-time. On the desktop, buy a better keyboard first—it's more effective to throw some cash at the problem than to tank your productivity for two months.

Strength

I've seen tremendous benefit from strength training and decent diet: my back stopped hurting, forearm pain from typing is long gone, and I'm in better condition for everything *else* in life, too. It may seem counterintuitive that deadlifts would reduce back pain or kettlebells would reduce forearm pain, but strong muscles hurt less.

There's nothing fancy to getting strong: look for an old-school strength coach to get you started.

Actions

Evaluate your workstation. How well does the keyboard fit? Mouse? Monitor? Find out how much the company will reimburse to improve things that aren't up to par. Decide how much of your own cash you should put in, if needed.

Learn to touch-type properly. Really, I mean it. Commit to getting those fingers on the home row and, one month from now, not needing to look at the keyboard *at all*.

CHAPTER 4

Teamwork

Some programmers are successful as a one-person company. The vast majority of us, however, need to play nice with others.

Much of what you'll do in the professional world requires interacting regularly with others. The introverted programmer might rather hole up in their cube and write code instead. However, your ability to interact effectively can accelerate—or limit—the coolness of the code you get to hole up with.

These "soft skills" aren't what programmers are known for, and this chapter won't make you a Dale Carnegie.[1] Instead, it's focused on hitting the high points of appreciating people's personality traits and how they interact in professional contexts.

The golden rule "Do to others what you would have them do to you" applies to teamwork, too. I'll add to that:

- In Tip 21, *Grok Personality Types*, on page 135, we look at some objective measures of personality. When you understand your own biases, and how others are different from you, it's easier to work with them.

- Tip 22, *Connect the Dots*, on page 141 then investigates the connections between people, because the company org chart only gives you a coarse picture of *authority*, and what's more interesting is a chart of *influence*.

---

1. Author of *How to Win Friends and Influence People*

- Tip 23, *Work Together*, on page 144 gets much more specific about programming, and collaborating, within your team.

- Finally, Tip 24, *Meet Effectively*, on page 148 gives you action items for collaboration-gone-wrong, the much-dreaded corporate meeting.

Tip 21

Grok Personality Types

[*Brown Belt*] Appreciating personality differences will help you work more effectively with others.

One thing about personalities is obvious: *not everyone is like you*. But perhaps not so obvious is that there are various *measures* of personality that can quantify just how much everyone is not like you.

One very common measure is known as the *Myers-Briggs Type Indicator,*[2] which measures how people perceive the world and make judgments. You can take a test to determine your MBTI, and it would certainly be handy to know the MBTIs of people you work with, but those are luxuries you probably won't get.

What's more important is to understand the factors Myers-Briggs—or other personality measurements—and use those to assess the people around you based on observation. You may not guess their types exactly, but you can get close enough. If you get a rough picture of how *you* deal with the world and how *they* deal with it, it can help you to relate to that person in a meaningful way.

Temperament: Introversion/Extroversion

The first type measurement is the scale between introversion and extroversion: inward-facing vs. outward-facing. These are terms you've likely heard before, and you can probably put yourself on the scale quite readily. In very general terms:

- Introverts recharge their batteries with alone or one-on-one time; engaging with a larger group drains their energy. They seek depth of knowledge and apply intellect before action.

---

2.   http://en.wikipedia.org/wiki/Myers-Briggs_Type_Indicator

- Extroverts recharge by spending time with people; alone they stagnate. They seek breadth of knowledge and apply action before intellectual reflection.

Introverts and extroverts can get along well when they appreciate each other's strengths. For example, programmers and salespeople tend to be polar opposites on this scale, but find two who respect each other and present a united front, and you have a force to be reckoned with. In fact, some of my best professional work was done in partnership with a business development guy—he'd herd the personalities; I'd take care of the technology side.

What's not so obvious about the I/E scale is that it's not the same thing as comfort in dealing with other people. We have a view of introverts as shy and extroverts as gregarious. That's not necessarily true. Introverts can be outgoing and expressive. Extroverts can be reserved.

I'm an introvert; I nearly pegged the scale in my MBTI test. However, as I've grown older, I've become much more outwardly expressive. This is partly a matter of training—trade shows are great for developing your skill in starting a conversation and quickly finding common ground with a complete stranger.

Perceiving: Sensing/Intuition

The next scale deals with how a person gathers data: sense (or data) driven vs. intuition and association. This parallels the L-mode and R-mode styles of thinking,[3] often referred to as "left brain" for linear and logical thought vs. "right brain" for pattern recognition and artistic skill. In general terms:

- People relying on sensing need to look at the data—possibly "data" from all five senses depending on what they're perceiving—and extract meaning from those sources. This is primarily an L-mode activity, using the sequential, reasoning part of their brain to put together the picture of what's going on.

---

3.   See *Pragmatic Thinking and Learning* [Hun08] by Andy Hunt.

- People relying on intuition will rely on less data but couple it with their instinctive reaction to the data they have. This isn't the same as a wild-ass guess—that *instinct* is coming from the brain, just another part. It's R-mode thinking, where the asynchronous, pattern-matching part kicks in and gives them that "flash" of insight.

The difference between these modes of thinking is exquisitely illustrated in Malcolm Gladwell's *Blink* [Gla06], where he discusses the ability of art experts to sniff out forgeries. Some take the sensing approach, going so far as to write software that brings statistics to bear on analyzing a suspect painting vs. a reference library of known authentic paintings, looking at details like stroke lengths and density. With enough data points, they can model a painter's style and sniff out fakes that may look visually identical—almost.

Other art experts can look at a suspect painting and intuitively *know* whether it's real or a fake. They're not just flipping a coin—whether they know it or not, they're using the pattern-matching engine in their brain, trained with decades of experience. In effect, they've built up their own statistical models. They can't tell you in rational terms how they do it; they just intuitively *know* a fake when they see it. And usually they're right.

How does this guide your interactions with others? Let's say you're trying to track down a bug. You're the data-driven type and you're working with an experienced co-worker who relies on intuition. If he says, "Hmmm… let's go poke in this other module" but can't explain why, try humoring him rather than pushing back. Just because he can't explain it doesn't mean there isn't real thought behind it—it's just thought from a different part of the brain than linear, logical thought. And if the hunch doesn't pan out, go collect some more data.

Note that most people tend to fall only mildly on one side or the other of this scale—they use components of both sensing and intuition on a regular basis.

Judging: Thinking/Feeling

What do you do once you've perceived the world around you? You take action. (Or go watch TV, but let's stick with the former.) This scale examines how you decide what action to take: logical analysis or empathy with the situation and people. Here are the characteristics of each:

- The person relying primarily on thought will look at the problem from the outside and reason through the best course of action. They may be a very caring and compassionate person, but their end decision is rooted more in logic than their feelings about the situation.

- The person relying on feeling puts themselves emotionally into situations, relating to people and circumstances on a more personal level. They may have tremendous reasoning horsepower, but they are fundamentally guided by their feeling about the *right* thing to do.

Programming comes with many straightforward situations where you have to think through a decision. I'm not talking about those situations. It's the ambiguous ones where this scale is meaningful. For example, you're working with another programmer to implement a feature, and you and she need to decide who does what.

The thinker's decision might go like this: we need to break apart the tasks so that each of us has a roughly equal load, we need to parcel out the tasks to the person who has the most expertise in each area, we need to make sure neither of us is stuck waiting on the other…

The feeler's decision, on the other hand, might go like this: I know she likes to work on database stuff and wants to do more of that, and the managers want to see visible progress on this feature soon because they're worried we can't pull it off, so I should rough out the user interface while she's doing the database part…

In a way, the judging scale is sort of the flip side of perceiving scale: there's how you see the world and what you do about it. However, the scales are indeed orthogonal: there are people who are sensing/feeling or intuition/thinking.

Programmers most likely fall largely on the thinking side of the scale, simply because we spend all day telling the computer how to make decisions based on data. Surely some of that seeps back into our own thought processes. However, don't discount the feeler's method of decision as inferior: in the big picture you're dealing with *humans* day in, day out, and some empathy with them will go a long way.

Lifestyle: Perception/judgment

The final scale indicates a preference between a person's perception mode vs. their judging mode. Obviously, everyone does some mix of perceiving and judging. You can't judge until you've perceived. However, when a situation doesn't need immediate judgment, does a person like to stay in perception mode or immediately move to judgment mode regardless of need?

- The perception-focused person likes to continue gathering input (either via sensing or intuition) and is OK with the situation staying undecided until a decision really needs to be made. They like to keep their options open, seeing no need to shut off additional opportunities for perception.

- The judgment-focused person likes to make a decision (either via thinking or feeling) and move on. Once they've perceived enough of a situation to make the call, leaving the situation open is just a source of stress.

This scale can be tremendously frustrating when two people don't recognize that they're on different ends of this preference. Let's say your manager falls on the judgment side, and you fall on the perception side. Your manager wants a decision on a certain technology to bring into the product. You'd rather keep it open since there's no immediate need to pick one vs. the other, and more time means more experience with the technologies in question.

Your boss gets frustrated, not understanding where you're coming from. He may consider you a slacker. He may lay down an artificial deadline. You, in turn, get equally frustrated. You think he's getting authoritarian. You think he's rushing a decision.

Really, all that's going on is a difference on the lifestyle scale. In a perfect world, you'd both recognize your different temperaments and compromise on making a decision timeline that gives you your perception time but still closes the decision before your manager gets overly stressed.

Common Combinations

If you think about the stereotypical programmer, all logic and no heart, you'd think of ISTJ: introverted, sensing, thinking, judgment. In fact, this is the most common combination for men in the United States, with an estimated 14 to 19 percent falling in this category.[4] The second-most common combination is ESTJ—the extroverted guy with all logic and no heart—comprising another 10 to 12 percent of U.S. men.

The women aren't dramatically different. ISFJ is most common with 15 to 20 percent, replacing the guy's thinking manner of judgment with feeling. ESFJ is another 12 to 17 percent. Sensing and judgment are most common across both sexes.

If you fall into one of the common categories, good news—odds are you won't have much trouble relating to the person next to you. On the other hand, if you're one of the outliers, recognize that early and understand that you'll need to put extra emphasis on relating to other personality types. Also, recognize that you may have a unique perspective on things—you may truly be the only person in the room who responds to a situation in the way you do.

Actions

Take the Myers-Briggs Type Indicator assessment. The test needs to be administered by a qualified tester. Your company's HR department may foot the bill—ask your manager.

See whether any of your friends have taken the MTBI assessment. Take your best guess before they tell you their type—were you right? Some of your friends might surprise you. If so, are there any clues that you should have picked up on? Try to figure out, for example, how to tell an expressive introvert apart from an extrovert.

---

4. http://www.capt.org/mbti-assessment/estimated-frequencies.htm

Tip 22

Connect the Dots

 [*Brown Belt*]   It takes a while to observe the connections between people. Further, you're best served by focusing on tasks when you're new to a job—influence will come later.

In Chapter 5, *Inside the Company*, on page 155 we discuss the *formal* authority of people, that is, how they're structured on an organizational chart. The real dynamics of influence are often different. The connections between people exert influence in ways that are hard to gauge when you're new to the team, and you won't find a diagram of them on the human resources website.

Let's consider the charts in Figure 7, *Formal and informal connections*, on page 142, where the top shows the formal connections between people in a fictional engineering department and the bottom shows some informal connections. Formally, Alice is the big cheese, Bob and Cathy are frontline managers, and the rest are programmers, testers, and so on.

Over time you'll discover the informal connections: Alice and Bob worked together at two prior jobs, so they have a strong bond of trust based on that experience. Holly, Ian, and Emma go out to lunch together every week, so they have a bond of friendship.

Dr. Karen Stephenson[5] studies these connections in a corporate environment. She goes into an organization, interviews its employees, and diagrams all these informal connections. Dr. Stephenson found that people tend to cluster, and there are key connections between clusters.

Some people are *hubs* that have connections to a lot of others. In our example, Frank is a hub—even though he's just a programmer, he has a lot of pals. Being a hub makes Frank

---

5.   http://www.drkaren.us/

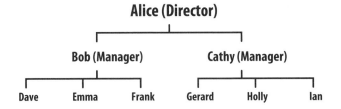

Figure 7—Formal and informal connections

an important connection point between the two teams since he has pals on both. Perhaps Dave gets stuck on a problem that Holly solved a week ago; Frank is the person who would tell Dave, "Hey, you should chat with Holly; I think she could help."

Another type of connection is the *gatekeeper*, a person who has a strong and unique connection to a key figure. Bob is a gatekeeper to Alice. Because of their long-standing professional relationship and Alice's lack of strong ties to others, Bob has a lot of informal pull with Alice—much more than his title would imply. Let's say Cathy is trying to start a new project within the department, but she knows it will be costly. She would be wise to convince Bob of its value because if *he* goes to Alice and says "Cathy has this great idea...," that carries a lot of weight.

The final connection is what Dr. Stephenson calls a *pulse-taker*, one who's on the periphery but knows a lot about what's going on. Dave could be a pulse-taker, because he's pals with both Bob (the gatekeeper) and Frank (the hub).

Dave's conversation with these two gives him a big-picture view of the department that neither Bob nor Frank have themselves.

If this sounds like high school all over again...well, it sort of is, because these connections are the normal social dynamics of any group. (Fortunately there's no homecoming dance to fret over.) What this means to *you* is that your co-workers have influence in ways that aren't obvious on your first day. An awareness of people's informal connections can give you insight—and eventually influence—even though you're low on the org chart.

Actions

Try your hand at playing Dr. Stephenson: start with the org chart as it exists formally. This may be on the company intranet, or you could ask your manager to draw it on your whiteboard.

Now ignore the org chart and start making a chart of connections. Mentally take note of day-to-day interactions like these:

- Groups of people who go out to lunch together.
- The folks who chat around the coffee pot in the morning.
- That one guy from the coffee pot group who then wanders cube to cube with his coffee, chatting with anyone he catches. (Every office has that guy.)
- The two programmers who always wind up at a whiteboard debating technical issues.
- The person your manager goes to when he's pissed off and needs to vent.

Based on these connections, can you identify any hubs, gatekeepers, or pulse-takers? I don't advocate using this knowledge to subversively try to exert influence—leave that to the salespeople—but rather use it in a constructive manner. For example, if you're stuck trying to figure out how to deploy code to a server and you don't know where to start, ask someone you've identified as a hub. They may not know the answer, but it's very likely they'll know who does know, and they can introduce you.

Tip 23

Work Together

 [*White Belt*] Your effectiveness as a programmer is, to a degree, gated by your ability to work with your team.

In most cases, you'll be one programmer among several, and like rowing a boat, the sum of efforts depends on everyone rowing the same direction. This is trite and easy to say. In practice, coordinating a programming effort is less like rowing a boat and more like herding cats.

Good programmers are opinionated and strong-willed. Ask any two programmers to solve a problem, and they'll solve it differently. Yet the product depends on several (or many) programmers working together and creating a cohesive whole.

Divide and Conquer

The average product requires many talents, and every programmer has unique skills, interests, and expertise. Understanding what *you* bring to the table is essential to contributing the most to the product.

When you're just starting out, your industry programming experience is zilch, but you have enthusiasm. OK, let's work with that. Is there a part of the product nobody else has experience in, either? This is usually in the gnarly parts; a common example is software packaging and field upgrade. It's a hairy mess, and nobody wants to touch it. It sounds like a good place to dig in and earn your stripes.

Taking on gnarly problems is how you build your expertise and credibility within the team. Sticking with easy parts of the project doesn't. (Balance this, however, with some early wins, as discussed in Tip 17, *Be Visible,* on page 110.) Look for credibility builders when the team is divvying up work;

where is an unmet need that you can tackle? Consider the following group planning meeting:

> *Manager:* *Any volunteers for the 3D flying icon rendering tool?*
>
> *Dave, Emma, Frank (in unison):* *Me.*
>
> *Manager:* *Now what about the part that imports 1986-vintage DXF files and converts them to our current format?*
>
> (crickets chirping)
>
> *You:* *If I take the lead on this one, can someone back me up if I get stuck?*
>
> *Frank:* *I wrote some DXF stuff a long time ago, and then my cat choked on the floppy disk containing the code, and I'm still very upset about that, but I should be able to help.*
>
> *You:* *OK, I'll take it.*

Now you have a gnarly project and also saved Frank—who would have gotten the assignment otherwise—from a month's worth of lament over the fate of his cat.

Pair Programming

Sometimes you set out to tackle a problem and it tackles you instead. No worries, it happens to all of us. Pair up with another programmer and try again. Often, a second set of eyes and a fresh perspective are all it takes to make the breakthrough you need.

Pair programming is effective enough that some teams *always* pair, one typing and the other observing and commenting. Other teams will work individually and pair only when someone gets stuck. I'll sometimes do a hybrid, with each person on a laptop in a common area, each attacking a different aspect of the problem.

If your team doesn't have an established practice for pairing, it's usually easy to get some time from a co-worker. Here are a couple tips:

- Try to find someone with experience in the area you're working in. ("Frank, I heard you know a thing or two about DXF. Could you watch over my shoulder for a bit and advise me on this gnarly part of the DXF importer?")

- If you need more than a few hours of time, run it by your manager. ("Can I borrow some of Frank's time? I'm in a tough spot and could use his help.")

The only unacceptable practice is floundering on your own, not asking for help. Yes, some problems require tedious investigation that takes a long time. Recognize, however, when you've gone past the point of diminishing return and it's time to get another set of eyes on the problem.

Concentration and Interruption

Collaboration necessarily involves both dividing work between individuals and working together. In most teams, this is a fluid thing, with unpredictable mixing of alone time and collaborative time. It's where those meet that can cause friction.

In programmer-speak, the "context switch overhead" required to flip between modes can be very high, depending on the person and the task at hand. Programming often requires intense concentration, and getting into that state — the *flow* or *zone* — takes time. This is why some companies give programmers offices to minimize interruptions.

On the other hand, collaboration requires interruption. This is why other companies put programmers in a large, open room to maximize collaboration. Both philosophies have truth to them, but you need to be conscious of the interplay between concentration and interruption to perform well in either environment.

First, when another team member is "in the zone," try not to bug them. Closed office doors or headphones are a good clue. When you need some in-the-zone time, turn off email, instant messaging, and your cell phone. If your company culture allows it, work from home or a coffee shop.

Second, get used to interruptions. There's tremendous value in collaboration, and shutting your office door shuts *you* out of the interactions going on around you. There are a number of productivity techniques you can use to minimize the impact of interruptions; *Getting Things Done* [All02] is a good place to start.

In the Center of Things

My very best working environment was precisely what most programmers dread: a low-wall cube in the middle of the office. I was a couple years into my career, and I wanted to sit with the main software team, so when a cube opened up—any cube—I grabbed it.

My new cube was right in the middle, by a common area. Interesting conversations would pop up, and I could participate effortlessly. I got involved with many parts of the product, gaining tremendous expertise and credibility very quickly. As it happens, the easiest way to get in the middle of things is to *physically* get in the middle of things.

I've been on the opposite end of the spectrum, too, working in my basement office a thousand miles away from the rest of my team. That was the worst job of my career—no matter what, I couldn't get into the action and participate in the design of the product.

Americans value the corner office with the window, but my own experience says the Japanese have it right: the most prized location—the location with the most influence—is the one in the center of things.

Actions

Here's an easy one: most of what we've been talking about boils down to *talking*. If you're in an office, make it a point to chat with another programmer each day. Coffee, lunch, and—in start-ups—dinner should provide ample opportunity to chat. If your company is physically distributed, get on instant messaging or the phone at least once a day.

The other part is dealing with interruptions. Take a survey of some productivity techniques—ask your co-workers, read some blogs, check out David Allen's book[6]—and pick one that you think meets your needs. Try it for four to six weeks; that's how long it takes to establish a new habit. If it's still more hassle than it's worth after that time, chuck it.

---

6. *Getting Things Done: The Art of Stress-Free Productivity* [All02]

Tip 24

Meet Effectively

 [*White Belt*]   You'll get invited to meetings from day one, so this is stuff you can use early —especially the bit about toilet flush timing.

Many consider meetings the bane of productivity; nowhere else can so many people waste so much time together. This isn't entirely untrue. However, meetings are necessary, and some are even productive.

The theory behind meetings is simple: decisions need to be made, so get the right people in a room, hash out the issues, and make a decision. In terms of "communication band-width," there's nothing more effective than a face-to-face talk. Email isn't very expressive and has high latency. Phone calls are somewhat more expressive, but it's easy for people to zone out. I've never been impressed with video confer-ences. Face-to-face is definitely the best way to communicate.

If talking directly with people is so effective, then, where do the meetings of endless tedium come from? You know, the cross-functional task forces on employee productivity? I sat through a meeting where twenty managers were involved with this critical question: do we discount some machines that have scratched covers, or do we spend the money to repaint the covers? Consider the cost of twenty managers' salaries for a fifteen-minute debate about paint. How much does a can of spray paint cost?

You'll be involved in some stupid meetings; just accept that. However, you can help keep meetings productive and, I hope, set a good example for others.

Having a Purpose

When you're invited to a meeting, consider what the orga-nizer is trying to get out of the meeting. Ideally that's stated clearly in the invitation. Most often it's not.

The No-Laptop Rule

Meetings used to be a lot more productive back in the 1990s when most people used desktop computers instead of laptops. Now, you'll get twenty people in a room and nineteen of them have their laptops open, checking their email or surfing the Web. Usually a handful of people will dominate the meeting with some trivium, and there's no incentive for them to care about wasting other people's time because the other people aren't paying attention anyway.

Some companies have recognized this and instituted a "no laptops in meetings" policy. It's a good idea, because when you get twenty people in a room with nothing but pen and paper to keep them entertained, they have incentive to get business done and get out of there.

Of course, there are valid exceptions: code reviews, product demos, and the like. The litmus test is that the laptop must make the meeting *more* efficient rather than less.

Let's say you're invited to a "cross-functional planning meeting" where you're supposed to "coordinate project activities" with other departments. That sounds like a noble cause, but *what do people actually have to do?* You can encourage a clearer purpose by asking the meeting organizer one-on-one, either in person or in email:

- Can you clarify the desired outcome of the meeting?

- What do I need to prepare ahead of time?

Don't be a smart-ass about it; keep your tone constructive. Remember, the organizer may not be responsible for this meeting monstrosity; they may be doing it just because they were told to do it. Your polite inquiry about outcomes and preparation will ideally nudge them to send out a *real* agenda.

Obviously, if it's *you* calling the meeting, ask yourself these questions ahead of time and use the answers as the basis for your agenda.

Having the Right Audience

Given a purpose, the other key ingredient is having the right people in the room. If you're looking for information, who has it? If you need a decision, who has the authority to make it? If it's a cross-functional task force, what functions do you forcefully want to cross?

You won't have much influence over the audience of other people's meetings, but you do have some control over *your* attendance. Don't just skip it; that's disrespectful. Instead, if you're invited to a monster meeting that you don't think you can contribute to, ask the organizer (again, one-on-one) if you need to attend.

Keep It Constructive

When you're in a meeting that devolves into whining and complaining, ask yourself whether can you nudge the conversation in a constructive direction. Here's an example:

> Dave: *The web servers can't handle that kind of load; they suck.*
>
> Emma: *No kidding, and the database server sucks, too.*
>
> (blah blah blah… more complaining here)
>
> You: *Is there another way we could solve the problem, like caching more pages to reduce the load?*

You don't have to come up with something brilliant; you just need to steer the conversation toward *solutions* rather than griping about *problems*. Programmers are great at dwelling on problems because, frankly, it's easy. Coming up with solutions—even if they don't pan out—requires talent.

Conference Calls

When meeting attendees are scattered over the globe, common practice is to get people on a conference call. There's nothing very special about these calls, but a couple tips may help. First, keep in mind that most people on a call are not paying full attention. If you need to ask someone a direct question, give them some lead-in: "I want to ask about our test suite. Bob, can you tell me about…" Assuming Bob is the test suite guy, that gives him a heads-up before you get to the meat of your question.

Second, mute your phone when not talking, especially if you're not paying full attention—it takes only one toilet flush to completely derail a call. (While I've never been guilty of the toilet flush myself, I have "attended" boring conference calls while laying in the bathtub.)

Actions

Try playing the role of meeting organizer. Surely, there's something about your project that could use feedback from others in the company. When you have something worth meeting about, try this:

1. Schedule the meeting for no longer than you think you need, even if it's just fifteen minutes.

2. Invite only the people you think need to attend; don't shotgun your address book.

3. Send out the agenda and the desired outcome one day ahead of time.

4. When the meeting is over, *it's over*—even if you didn't use all the time you scheduled. Thank people for their time and let them get back to work.

5. If appropriate, email meeting minutes to the attendees, paying particular attention to any commitments made. These "action items" let everyone know who's on the hook to *do something* about what was discussed in the meeting.

Even if the attendees aren't thrilled about going to another meeting, they'll be pleasantly surprised when you stick to the agenda, get what you need, and let them go.

Part III

The Corporate World

CHAPTER 5

Inside the Company

One of my favorite children's books is Richard Scarry's *What Do People Do All Day?* I still wonder that sometimes. As I write this, for example, IBM has 426,751 employees.[1] What do *they* do all day?

Well, let's aim a little lower.

I'll be honest; you don't need to know everybody. Many programmers never venture to the other parts of the building; they saw the "Now Entering Marketing: Two Drink Minimum" banner and thought it best to turn back.

That said, a master (and *master-to-be*) programmer benefits tremendously from a more-traveled perspective. Marketing and sales can tell you all about customers and how the product is selling with them. PR can tell you how the press is responding. Support can tell you what customers are complaining about.

This chapter has only two tips, but they're meaty ones:

- Tip 25, *Know Your Peeps*, on page 157 starts on your home turf. There are lots of roles within the engineering department besides the programmers. This tip covers the common ones and gives a few pointers on how to snag one of those roles for yourself.

- Then it's time to steel your confidence and trek into the lands previously unknown. Tip 26, *Know Your (Corporate) Anatomy*, on page 163 gives you the major landmarks outside of engineering: Where do press releases come

---

1.   http://www.ibm.com/ibm/us/en/

from? Who keeps the lights on? And why do I keep hearing that the sales guys have all the fun?

Tip 25

Know Your Peeps

 [*White Belt*]   You need perspective on your peers (and their roles) very early in the job.

Programming is *sometimes* a solo activity, like the coding cowboy who gets to call all his own shots. But for the vast majority of the time, it's a team of programmers building a product together, and you'll need to work in cooperation with others to be effective.

Roles

First let's talk about who's on your team and what they do. These roles vary depending on the company, and there may be specialist roles at your company that I don't discuss, but they usually go something like this.

Programmers

When most people think of "programmers," they think of nerds with thick glasses sitting at computers and typing industriously. While the glamour part is all true, the typing part is only half true — there's also a lot of nonprogramming time required to shepherd a product to completion. There's bug hunting, testing, meetings, and other duties. These vary tremendously depending on the organization and your product's development stage. (Hint: the bug hunt right before shipping *always* sucks.)

In an organization with minimal overhead — that is to say, programmers get to spend most of their time on design and implementation — this is quite a fun role. You must already be halfway convinced if you're reading this book. People can, and do, spend their entire career in this role. Progressive companies will pay super-senior programmers the same kind of money they pay directors and vice presidents.

There are lots of titles that go with this role: programmer, developer, software engineer, firmware engineer, and so forth. They're mostly the same. "Engineer" doesn't mean anything special in the software world, because there's no special qualifications for an engineer vs. a programmer. (This is different in fields that have licensing requirements, like civil engineering.) "Firmware engineer" is usually reserved for people working on embedded systems and operating system components.

If this is the role you want but it's not your first job, don't despair—you can get here. New product development requires experience, so it's usually necessary to prove yourself in another role first.

Tech Leads

A technical lead is just a programmer with some official blessing to call the shots on technical matters. Frequently a team with five or more programmers will have a tech lead who has expertise in the problem domain or a track record of good leadership. This person is not, however, a manager with the authority to hire or fire.

Since this role is usually earned within the organization—as opposed to being hired in from the outside—tech leads tend to have solid experience and sound judgment. You would do well to ask one to mentor you, as in Tip 15, *Find a Mentor*, on page 103.

To get to this role yourself, you have to pay your dues. It usually takes several years of solid work and informal team leadership to attain this role.

Architects

The architect title has two distinct meanings. In some companies, the architect is considered an analyst who collects product requirements and drafts a detailed design document that other programmers are supposed to go implement. Then the architect receives a hefty consulting fee and leaves.

In other companies, the architect is just a team lead—someone who has demonstrated a knack for leadership and design. This architect sticks with the product through its development. There's no free pass to create a design and leave—he has to eat his own dog food.

There are additional titles that boil down to the same thing: chief scientist, fellow, and whatnot. These honorifics are generally bestowed on a very small handful of people at large companies.

Managers

Now we're stepping outside the realm of technical leadership and into the management ranks—the folks who do the hiring, firing, and performance reviews.

Programming managers come in two varieties: those who are managers by trade—we call these "people managers"— and those who used to be programmers. Both have advantages. Good people managers may not understand the technology, but they do understand team dynamics, such as how to hire the right team and get them working together well. (My very best manager was a people manager.)

Managers who used to be programmers are a mixed bag. Some of them, frankly, would rather be programming but got promoted into management, usually because they were good technical leaders. This kind of manager is great at guiding you on programming issues, but you'll need to look elsewhere for guidance on long-term career issues. You may want to find a more people-skilled mentor to help you on that side, as discussed in Tip 15, *Find a Mentor*, on page 103.

If you want to move into management, consider that you won't program anymore; you'll spend your time on project planning, personnel, budget, and so forth. It's a very different job. However, if you have the people skills and you want more authority within the company, management could be right up your alley.

Testers

Testers are responsible, obviously enough, for testing the product before it gets released to customers. However, there's a lot of ways to test a product and therefore a lot of variation in how testers do their job. At the simplest, they read the user guide and poke around in the user interface. At more advanced levels, they write automation scripts and programs to do the testing for them—they're not that different from programmers.

Testers and programmers often have an antagonistic relationship. Programmers can get offended when testers find bugs, but the programmer needs to remember that a bug found in-house is far better than a bug found in the field. Testers can consider it a victory to find a bug, but the tester needs to remember that bugs are not victories to revel in; they are failures. Both roles need to remember that they're playing on the same team and share a common goal: to ship a high-quality product.

Testing is a common job for inexperienced new-hires. If you're in this role and you were hoping for a programming job instead, don't worry—testing has its plus side. You get to see the product from the end user's perspective, and this perspective is easily lost at the programmer's point of view. When it comes to the company's bottom line, end-user value is the only value that counts.

To move into programming, the path is straightforward: program your way out. Automate manual tests, build test tools, and do anything that involves writing code. In every company I've seen, testers who can program, without fail, get sucked into programming.

Build/Deployment

Larger engineering organizations may have dedicated people for builds and tools. These folks have highly specialized skills with version control, automation tools, packaging tools, and release processes. They also get very grumpy when you break the build—one build master I worked with had a tomahawk she named Bad Mojo, and you didn't want to see the two of them walking toward your cube.

Another related specialization is deployment. Products that run on hundreds or thousands of servers require a special level of care and automation to keep them running. These people make sure that new code will deploy correctly, roll it out in stages, and manage any problems that come up. This may look like system administration on the surface, but it's far more technical; the issues with staged deployment (and possible rollback) with thousands of servers could easily be more difficult than the application itself.

To put these technical specializations in perspective, consider a company that operates servers at Google's scale. Some of Google's most advanced software are tools to help programmers distribute workload across the cluster or work with data at the petabyte scale.

Your Role on the Team

Your first job won't be chief architect of a new product. You'll get grunt work because, from square one, you need to start on small things before you'll be trusted with large things. It's a natural cycle as old as the craft trades; apprentices need to work their way up.

A manager of mine put it this way: if you're a silversmith's apprentice, you won't start on casting; you'll start on something much less glamorous, like filing. You get cast parts from the master and file down the rough edges. When you have that down, you can try your hand at casting. Of course, your first molds and casts will suck—meaning you'll have a lot of rough edges to file down afterward. Then you see firsthand, *ah-ha*, the better I make the mold and pour the cast, the less filing I have to do!

In the same way, the budding programmer may start on something like testing. You'll have to tediously figure out how to test various parts of the code to make sure they work. Then when you get moved up to writing some code—along with their tests—you'll be motivated to write modular code that's easy to test. If you don't, it's only yourself that you're punishing.

So, don't get discouraged when you enter the workforce with wide eyes and idealism, only to get some role you think is crummy. You won't be there forever; you just need to work your way to the role you want.

Actions

If you're not yet in the professional world, you'll have to file this one away for future use.

- *Step 0:* Get a job.

- *Step 1:* Go chat with some of your teammates and figure out what they do. There's often a difference between a person's *title* and *what they do*. Alice and Bob may both have the title "software developer," but Alice may be the database expert and Bob is the Unix guru. Simply introduce yourself and ask what someone is working on; with some time, you'll figure out people's specialties.

- *Step 2:* Based on what you've seen people in your team doing, what looks the most interesting to you? Write down what *you* want to be doing in a couple years.

- *Step 3:* Brainstorm some short-term actions you could take to get you closer to your goal. Pick three and act on them over the next six months.

Tip 26

Know Your (Corporate) Anatomy

[*Brown Belt*]   For your first year you don't need to know what marketing does. Once past that, it's time to broaden your perspective.

Like people, every company will have its own personality, but they all tend to have the same basic building blocks. At a technology company, engineering tends to have a medieval view of their place in the corporate universe: "everything revolves around us." However, it's important to understand that engineering is just one part of the company; there are parts that are just as essential to the company's success. "Now the body is not made up of one part but of many…If one part suffers, every part suffers with it; if one part is honored, every part rejoices with it."[2]

The first step in figuring out your company's structure is to dig up an organizational chart. Look on the corporate intranet for something that looks like Figure 8, *Abbreviated org chart*, on page 164 and use that to follow along with the discussion. Since we discuss the engineering organization in Tip 25, *Know Your Peeps*, on page 157, it's the one group not covered here.

Along the way I'll include *conversation starters* that can help break the ice with people in other departments. If you're naturally social, you won't need them. In all cases, improvise away.

Administrative Assistants

This isn't an organization *per se* but rather a role that shows up in many departments. The assistants are assigned either to busy executives or to groups, and they handle all kinds of stuff: scheduling, event planning, answering/placing phone calls, booking travel, and much more.

---

2.   1 Corinthians 12:14-26

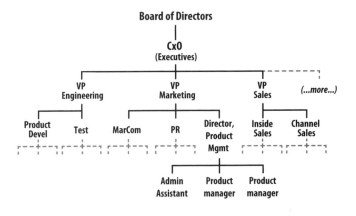

Figure 8—Abbreviated org chart

These are people you *need to know* because they can help with all kinds of stuff when you're in a jam. Need to file an expense report but can't figure out how to submit your receipts? Need to ask the CTO a question about your project but her calendar is booked solid? Need to find a conference room that you've never heard of before? There's an AA who can help.

Several times I've known an AA who was later promoted to a position of relative power. Disrespect an administrative assistant at your own peril.

Support

The first time a product goes out the door, the company needs an end-user support team. As a programmer, you'll need to help them do their jobs. The support tech gets a call with some vague description of "the program crashed" or "the website spits out an error," and this may be the first time the problem has been seen. Guess who's job it is to dig into the code and figure out what went wrong? Lucky you.

Support is usually broken into several tiers: tier one is responsible for logging the customer's problem, verifying the customer has a support contract, and other (mostly) nontechnical stuff. They may have a script of common troubleshooting questions they run through. (Chances are

Industry Perspective: Not Just Administrative

Be sure to make friends with your administrative assistant (AA). It may seem tangential, but that individual runs far more of the show than you realize and is heavily wound into the fabric of the company. AAs are largely ignored—especially by techies —but you will run across them *forever*. Remember, they're on a job path too—an easy and good relationship now may well pay huge dividends in the future. Help this along by showing up at your AA's desk at times other than when you need something.

—*Mark "The Red" Harlan, engineering manager*

you've been on the receiving end of one of these scripts. *"Yes, I tried rebooting my computer already!"*)

Tier two and up is where the geeks live. When rebooting doesn't solve the problem, the call gets bounced to tier two. While they may not have programming skills, they usually have very good troubleshooting skills and lots of institutional knowledge. "Oh, that error 96 usually means their frombazzle driver is down-rev; we've seen that before."

As a programmer, the best thing you can do to help the support team is to make the product give them the details they need to troubleshoot a problem. "Segmentation fault" is not an error message the support person can work with. However, a detailed message that the customer can email to support is very valuable. Remember, if you don't help support troubleshoot the problem, some unlucky programmer—like *you*—is going to have to troubleshoot it.

Note that it's easy for the support staff to get disillusioned with the product they're supporting. Understand their position: they get calls all day long from people who are having problems with the product. The people who are using the product just fine don't call to say, "Just letting you know; all's good here, and I'm happy." The support staff has a skewed perception of the product's quality. Don't let this infect your outlook.

Conversation Starters

You may not need any conversation starters for support; they may come beating down *your* door. Consider yourself lucky if you get to start the conversation on your own terms. Here are a few ways to open:

> You: Hi, I work on [Product x]. What have you been hearing from the field lately about it?

You might get an earful in return. Don't feed the fire; instead, follow with something constructive:

> You: What are some ways the product could help make your job easier?

Finally, if you make pals with a tier-two or three support person, I suggest the following:

> You: Would you mind if I sat in on a few calls or listened to some recorded ones?

These folks are talking to end users of your product all day long—wouldn't you like to hear what the users are saying? Keep in perspective, however, that these are only the users who are having problems. Don't let it beat you down.

Marketing

Engineers tend to have a dim and distorted view of marketing. Most engineers also don't know what marketing actually *does*. Let's fix that.

The overall goal of the marketing department is to influence people's perceptions about your company and the stuff it sells. Those people include both customers and the press. In a good marketing organization, the feedback from people —the *market*—also drives the development of new products and services.

Marketing Communications (aka MarCom)

This is what most people think of when they think of "marketing." MarCom does the advertising, the product brochures, the logos, and so forth. The typical sarcastic response to marketing communications is that they're there to put lipstick on a pig. But really their role is to put lipstick on whatever the engineering team gives them. If it's a pig, then what choice do they have?

Another thing to keep in mind is that marketing communications wants to make the product look good *to the customer*.

Your perception of the product's value and the customer's perception of value are probably very different. Before you complain that MarCom ignored the feature you spent a year working on, remember that a lot of engineering features aren't *directly* relevant to the customer; they're part of the supporting cast that makes the end-user features possible.

Public Relations

Where the MarCom team is primarily interested in communicating to potential customers, the PR team is responsible for talking with press and analysts. Chances are you won't interact much with PR; however, you'll see their *press releases* on your company's website.

The press release will say lots of glowing things about, for example, your latest product. There will be some made-up quotes from executives and information on your company. If you think the press release sounds corny, remember you are not the target audience; *it's for the press.*

To a writer at some industry trade magazine, press releases are a constant stream of "here's what happened today," and they'll cherry-pick some to write about. They need tidbits on what's new and some quotes for emphasis. The press release gives them this raw material. The writer (supposedly) puts their own spin on it and *voila!*—news is made.

Product Management

This team's role varies greatly from company to company. A classic product manager is responsible for determining market needs and specifying what the product should do to meet those needs—this a product's strategy. When engineering gets the directive "the product needs to do *[x],*" that's usually coming from a product manager.

In the technology world, however, the product strategy is sometimes determined by engineering management, and the resulting product is pushed into marketing. In this environment, the product manager sticks to more tactical tasks such as supporting MarCom and sales.

Some product managers come from programming backgrounds; this can be a uniquely strong role for a person who's skilled in building products *and* can see the technology

Industry Perspective: Market First, Technology Second

Product managers document the customer needs and the problems—as opportunities—in the market. Engineers are "problem solvers" and are quick to jump into solutions. Someone with a marketing background usually realizes they should not cross that line—a product manager needs to thoroughly *understand* the problem without trying to solve it.

–Jim Reekes, product manager, The 280 Group

from the customer's point of view. If that sounds interesting to you, we'll discuss it further in Tip 33, *Find Your Place*, on page 222.

Conversation Starters

Knowing a few people in marketing is the first step to understanding the customers you build products for. First and foremost, know your product's product manager. Here's a simple intro:

> You: Hi, I work on [Product X]. Can you tell me some of the ways customers use the product?

Don't just talk about features; talk about customers and their needs. Product managers get frustrated by engineers who endlessly talk about features without understanding the customer first.

MarCom folks are promoting the product, so ask about that:

> You: What's the next marketing campaign you're working on?

Or perhaps:

> You: How do you think our customers perceive our company?

In the case of PR, substitute "the press" in place of customers.

Sales

At first glance, it would appear that salespeople are mostly skilled at looking good in suits. Get to know them better, and you'll find they're also good at drinking and eating steak. For this reason, when you're at a trade show and it's the end of the day, *go find a sales guy chatting up an important*

Marketing Is You, Too

There may be a whole department at your company called "marketing," but the truth is, *everyone* at the company represents the company. When you're at a trade show wearing the company logo, *you* influence your company's image with everyone you meet. When you're in a mailing list conversation about some programming nugget and your email address ends with your-company.com, you influence your company's image with everyone who reads that email.

In all those interactions, do you project the image you should? You're a professional, and your image should reflect that. Whatever strife or arguments you may have within the company, *leave that out* of your dealings with the outside world. While programmers get paid to write good code and not to look pretty, the company still expects you to act like a pro while representing them.

customer and get into the conversation. That way, he'll invite you along, and you'll get to drink and eat steak on his expense account.

The nature of sales depends a lot on the company's products and business model. If your company sells direct to customers, you may have a *direct sales* team that does just that. Many companies sell through distributors or value-added resellers; thus, they'll have a *channel sales* team to manage that business. Other companies may have a *business development* team that develops more strategic relationships with other companies.

In all cases, if you wonder what motivates a sales guy, find out about his compensation plan. Most all salespeople make meager salary but have big financial incentives tied to their performance. It's not that the sales guys are a bunch of money-grubbing scoundrels, it's that they have to bring home the moolah, or they'll wind up making less than a McDonald's fry cook. If *your* contribution to the company's top line could be measured so readily, the company might motivate *you* in a similar manner, too.

Sales performance, as with company performance, is usually tracked by quarter and by year. Don't screw with a sales guy near the end of March, June, September, and December.

On the flip side, if you're asked to talk to a customer or give a demo and you help the sales guy land a deal, you'll have a pal for life (or at least until next quarter).

Conversation Starters

Salespeople are the easiest people in the world to start a conversation with. You probably won't have to say a word; they'll start the conversation for you—it's what they do best. In the rare case that you need to take the initiative, here's one surefire way:

> You: *Want to go out for a beer?*

I'm joking, sort of—just introduce yourself and ask how sales are going this quarter. Also ask what parts of the product are most compelling to customers. Programmers focus on what's cool; the sales team can tell you what customers really *pay for*, which may be very different.

One thing to keep in mind is that talking to the average salesperson requires some bravado. They speak boldly and confidently—again, that's what they do best—so it's easy for them to dominate the conversation. If you're not so outgoing, toughen up and don't let their bluster intimidate you.

Information Technology

Known by many names: information technology (IT), management information support (MIS), and so forth. These are the people who manage the company's computing infrastructure: the computers and network. This work varies from simple (keeping inventory) to very hard (tuning a clustered database). If your company's product is a computing service, for example, cloud compute hosting, then you may have separate groups for general company IT needs and product-specific IT.

Note that the role of Unix system administrator has a history and lore to it. The role, epitomized by the Bastard Operator From Hell (BOFH[3]), is a cantankerous uber-sysadmin who will p0wn any luser who gets in his way. Unfortunately, the BOFH is much less common these days, having been replaced by more point-and-click Windows sysadmins.

---

3. http://en.wikipedia.org/wiki/Bastard_Operator_From_Hell

They're too weary from pointing and clicking to be devious and evil like the BOFH of the past.

If system administration is your first job out of school, be careful not to get pigeonholed here. When you apply for a programming job and what you have on your resume is sysadmin, many hiring managers will trash your resume before they notice your computer science degree.

Conversation Starters

First, make sure you understand one thing about the IT guy: Unix or Windows. The easy way to tell is to look at their bookshelves:

Unix:

> *GNU Emacs, DNS and BIND, sendmail*…or no books at all, just a tomahawk. (Warning: in the latter case, you've probably dealing with a BOFH, so tread carefully.)

Windows:

> *Windows Server Administration, Active Directory Administration, SQL Server Administration,* and so forth (each about six inches thick).

That established, here's how you might chat up a Unix sysadmin:

> You: *What's your favorite Linux distribution?*

Or Windows:

> You: *Have you tried the latest PowerShell?*

Obviously you'll need to improvise here for current technologies. Specifically, do *not* go over to IT and start whining about the Internet connection or email server if you're trying to make friends.

Facilities

You'll see people from the facilities team roaming the building on a regular basis. You'll need their help when moving offices or cubes, and they're also the folks to contact when a toilet is flooding and threatening to take out the server room. *Every* facilities guy I've met has been gruff and grumpy on the outside, and you can understand why: all day long they get calls about toilets flooding. Wouldn't you be grumpy too?

However, the same grumpy facilities guys I've known have also been very laid back once I got to know them. Just be cool and show them some respect. Why is it good to have allies in facilities? For one thing, they're much more likely to "look the other way" when they catch you working on a office prank. I was once standing on a conference room table with a bunch of ceiling tiles popped out, with spools of wire and tools at my feet, rewiring an office intercom speaker. Our facilities guy, Yer, came wandering through:

Me: *Hi, Yer, how's it going?*

Yer: *Ummm... (puzzled look) going fine...anything wrong?*

Me: *No, no, not at all. You didn't see anything here, OK?*

Yer: *No problem. (walks off)*

Conversation Starters

Honestly, I've always gotten to know the facilities people with a simple "Hi, how's it going?" as I run into them. They're always wandering the building, so those encounters come up often. Then you'll surely run into something truly bizarre—fried squirrel in the building's power transformer, for example—and have a good opportunity for a real conversation. Be sure to ask about the most bizarre thing they've seen on the job.

Manufacturing

You'll have a manufacturing department only if your company makes hardware (obviously), and even then it's likely the manufacturing will be halfway around the world. You may have a model shop in-house, however, for building prototypes.

I enjoy making pals with the model shop folks, partly because it's tremendous fun to run a mill. Also, there's usually someone who can rework circuit boards with surface-mount parts, which takes tremendous skill. If you work on hardware, you *will* fry a board, and these people can usually fix it.

If you have manufacturing in-house, it's likely you'll get roped into debugging problems that show up on the assembly line when a product enters production. It takes a while to get the kinks worked out of building a new product at production scale. Tip: during development of a hardware product, you always write isolation tests for various hardware components—*leave those in*, hidden if need be, because they'll be useful on the manufacturing line.

Conversation Starters

On manufacturing floors there's a lot going on, and it can be hard to *not* get in the way. Because of this, I'd ask your manager to take you on a tour. Find the line lead for your product and start with something like this:

> You: *I've always been curious how these go together. What's the hardest part about building this product?*

I've found tremendous value in checking in with manufacturing from time to time. Little decisions from engineering can have big impacts on the manufacturing floor; you might be shocked at the stuff these guys and gals have to put up with when building your stuff. You'll uncover opportunities for easy product improvements that can save manufacturing a lot of hassle.

Human Resources

The first person you talked to at your company was probably in human resources (HR). They do the legwork on setting up interviews and moving the hiring process along. While they don't make the final decision to hire, they *will* tell the hiring manager if you act like a jerk. Just follow along with the process and be polite.

HR also manages the benefits package: your health insurance, 401(k), and related stuff. Feel free to ask questions about these things; they're complex, and you need to understand what you're signing up for.

The other duty of HR is to mediate the process of employee conflicts. However, if you have a problem with a co-worker, *do not go to HR first*. When HR is notified of a conflict, it starts a process rolling that can spiral way past your intent. Talk to the co-worker or your manager instead. When HR gets involved, that's when people start getting fired. The vast majority of problems are best solved without going nuclear.

Of course, if the conflict is serious—harassment, violence, that kind of thing—then it's time to go to HR. Be aware that many levels of management will get involved and jobs will be on the line.

Conversation Starters

You won't need any help here; HR will be your first point of contact with a company, and they'll also get you started on day one.

Finance and Accounting

Now we're really getting outside the realm of your day-to-day interaction. This domain gets very complicated very fast, so I'll stick to the two-minute overview.

First, *finance* and *accounting* are two different things. Finance is focused on the future: budgeting and securing money for product development. Accounting is focused on the present and past: how the business performed and where all the money went.

Second, businesses don't treat money like you treat your checking account. You can look at a receipt from the ATM machine and know how much money you have in the bank. A business, on the other hand, *breathes* money like a living being—there is constantly money flowing in and out. The accounting folks generate two key documents that show the health of the company: the *profit and loss statement* that is a snapshot in time of the company's money, and a *cash-flow statement* that shows more of the dynamic flow of money.

Why should you care? For starters, the executives are *always* rah-rah-rah about the company's potential, right up to the "We ran out of money today" speech where everyone gets laid off. The numbers from the accountants, however, don't lie (unless there's some real shady stuff going on). Ask your manager if you can see the P&L and cash-flow statements. In a privately held company, you may not get to see them. In a public company, they're freely available; it's required by law.

I'll be frank; I don't look at these documents often. It takes education to make heads or tails of them, and if you want to know how the product is selling, it's a lot easier to ask a product manager. The numbers, however, give you a raw, unfiltered perspective on where the company stands, and it's good to see them at least once.

Conversation Starters

Let me come clean; I have no idea how to start a conversation with a finance person. I'm even friends with one. I'm not sure how that happened.

On the surface, finance seems like the most boring job in the world, and the finance folks know it. They usually can't articulate their attraction to the field. To a programmer, though, there's a parallel that might help you relate: a good finance person understands the flow of money through a company like you understand the flow of data through a computer. Have you ever visualized the flow of a complex program in your head? They do that with things like money and credit.

I've failed you on a good conversation starter here, but trust me, getting to know a finance person can be quite interesting. Just don't ask them to help you with your taxes—that's their equivalent to "Oh, you're a programmer, can you help me fix my computer?"

The Executives

Executives come in many flavors, and their titles vary depending on the company. We'll look at some of the most common.

One thing to keep in mind is that these are the *officers* of the company, which has some specific ramifications—especially with companies whose stock is publicly traded—since they are considered the ultimate insiders. For example, they can't sell stock except for very specific windows of time, as governed by the SEC.

Since the officers of the company give the orders, they are also the ones who ultimately need to answer for any major screw-ups. The "I didn't know" excuse doesn't fly since they're supposed to know everything that's going on. These are high-stress jobs.

Chief Executive Officer (CEO)

The CEO is the big cheese; decisions from here cannot be over-ruled. The CEO is responsible for the company at a strategic (big-picture) level and ultimately the company's success.

I've observed two main types of CEOs in high-tech companies: the founder and the numbers guy. The founder is one who has been with the company from the start and truly "gets" the vision of the company and its products. If the company was funded by venture capital, chances are this founder will get ousted within two to five years. The numbers guy comes in second. He's known for execution (delivering product, making money) and generally doesn't give a damn about vision or products—he's there to make sure the investors get their money's worth.

Both styles have their advantages. Obviously the founder CEO is more inspiring to work for. The numbers CEO is going to be more reliable for making sure your paycheck doesn't bounce. Personally I prefer to take my chances with the founder.

If you get an opportunity to talk with the CEO, by all means take it. Most CEOs who are worth anything are curious to hear how things are going in the trenches—they're so busy with the other executives that it's a rare opportunity for them to get the lowdown directly from a programmer.

Chief Technology Officer (CTO)

This is the lesser-cheese but the most important one to *you*. The CTO is responsible for the company's technology development. She can be execution-oriented or may be more of a visionary; again, both have their benefits.

I highly recommend talking with the CTO at some point; just email and say you'd like a bit of her time to chat when she's free. Ask about where she sees the company's technology going and where the market is going. In turn, the CTO will probably ask you how things are going in the trenches. Be honest, and maybe brag a little about something cool you've done lately.

One thing to beware: most CTOs came up through the ranks—they've been programmers before—so don't try to B.S. this person. Just tell things straight, even when it's not good news.

Chief Information Officer (CIO)

Not all companies have a CIO. This executive is responsible for all the information within the company, not product development. The CTO is about product, the CIO is about information. For example, if you have massive databases that contain hard-won proprietary info (say customer or financial data), the CIO is responsible for protecting it and using it to the business's full advantage.

If you're working on a data mining project, chances are that came from the CIO. Most companies don't have a problem with collecting data—they can collect data at a prodigious rate. The problem is making sense of it. This sometimes goes by the name of *business intelligence,* and if you're good at statistics, you could become the CIO's hero.

Chief Operations Officer (COO)

Operations is all about getting stuff done. It's one thing to have great ideas or great data; it's another thing entirely to keep a whole company running smoothly. The COO is responsible for the day-to-day operations of pretty much everything. A good COO can take a lot of burden off the other executives, freeing the CEO to focus on business strategy and CTO to focus on product strategy. Without a COO, they spend a lot of time just trying to figure out what the heck is going on across the company.

Chief Financial Officer (CFO)

This is the executive who knows everything about the company's money, both where things are at now (the accounting side) and how they're going to fund projects that are underway (the finance side).

Chief Legal Officer (or General Counsel)

All the companies I've worked at have had a general counsel instead of a CLO. Same thing: this is the head lawyer. Most any business arrangement that needs "the i's dotted and the t's crossed" will cross the general counsel's desk.

You may interact with the general counsel to go over software licenses. These days, it's increasingly common to integrate open source software when building a technology product, and the sharp GC will ask about the licenses for each component. It makes everybody's life easier if someone on the team tracks these (for example on a wiki page) for easy reference when the lawyers come calling. If *you're* the one who has been tracking licenses, you're the one who will sit down with the GC (and probably CTO) to go over them before the product ships. It's an easy opportunity to get executive-level visibility.

Chief [x] Officer

There are lots of other officers who could exist at your company: security, compliance, dog washing, and so on. For these specialist roles you'll need to ask your manager what they do.

Board of Directors

Not all companies will have a board of directors. Mom-and-pop shops won't have one. When investors start to pile money into a company, however, they demand some level of oversight, and this is where the board comes into play. In publicly held companies, the board is elected by the shareholders.

The board isn't involved with day-to-day decisions; in fact, they generally meet only once a quarter. The board meeting is where the executives (company officers) present how the business did last quarter and what they're planning for next quarter.

Since the board of directors is there to represent the shareholders, most board members don't work for the company. They could come from investment firms (that is, strictly money guys), or they could be executives at companies in related businesses (that is, domain experts). The latter, especially, are there to provide advice to the executives and also call B.S. if the company is doing something stupid.

If there's one thing the CEO is scared of, it's the board of directors. If they don't think the CEO is leading the company well—in other words, protecting the investments and interests of the shareholders—they will bring in someone new.

Actions

Throughout this tour of the company we've encountered a lot of people to talk to. Your assignment, should you choose to accept it, is to go start some conversations with people outside of engineering. Start close to home, with test and support. Then branch out, for example with the product manager for the product you work on. Before long you'll get introduced to plenty of others and discover the rest of the org chart organically.

Along the way, keep in mind Tip 22, *Connect the Dots*, on page 141. Notice how these connections spider throughout the company—and you'll discover why the administrative assistants hold so much power.

CHAPTER **6**

Mind Your Business

Many programmers fear an MBA—the master of business administration. These are people who will corner you by the watercooler and tell you about seed funding, venture capital, and stock option dilution. *Run!*

But the truth is, the master programmer has to know a thing or two about business. Much like our investigation into other roles within the company, it pays to understand the context of your work: When is my product going to ship? Who's going to buy it? How does the company make money from it?

As a programmer, most of your contribution is toward the product. This chapter, accordingly, takes a product-heavy bias. Even if you program internal systems—for example, the trading software used by an investment firm—you can consider your software a product whose customers happen to be inside the company.

I'm not looking to give you an MBA, of course. We'll cover just the high points you'll want early in your career:

- We start with your first, most pressing issue: Tip 27, *Get with the Project*, on page 183 focuses on practical advice for estimating and scheduling your work. Time is money, and the company tracks both closely.

- Tip 28, *Appreciate the Circle of (a Product's) Life*, on page 189 looks at the product as it evolves over time. Your job looks a bit different depending on where your product currently lives within this cycle.

- Then we get into purely business matters. Tip 29, *Put Yourself in the Company's Shoes,* on page 200 addresses what the company is doing and why we programmers have jobs.

- Finally, something the MBA's b-school doesn't like to admit, Tip 30, *Identify Corporate Antipatterns,* on page 203 points out some recurrent patterns of business gone wrong.

Tip 27

Get with the Project

 [*White Belt*] Before you write a line of code, someone will be asking you how long it'll take.

"Are we there yet?"

On the family road trip, your dad may have quipped that it's the journey, not the destination, that you should focus on. That's not the case for your project manager.

It turns out there's a lot of ways to answer that question. Software projects are notoriously hard to estimate, and the industry moves so fast that a product's specification rarely stays the same for even a month—this is why many teams have given up on writing specs. So, the answer to "Are we there yet?" is often something between "No" and "It depends on what your definition of *there* is."

Our industry has put considerable effort into estimating software projects because there's a lot of money at stake: the company makes a gamble on each project, estimating how much money it'll make vs. how much money it spends. When the project schedule blows up, the company's cost blows up as well. Plus, there's the cost of lost business. Plus, opportunity cost…you get the idea.

The project manager's job is to plan and execute the project. This person knows what needs to be done and knows where things stand right now. It's not his job, however, to define the project's goals—that belongs to the product manager and company stakeholders. It's also not his job to manage the people. To you, the project manager is the guy who hounds you every week, asking "Are we there yet?"

Waterfall Project Management

The traditional method of managing software projects is to manage them just like any other engineering project:

Project vs. Product Management

Many people confuse *project* and *product* management. They're very different:

Project management is about scheduling and tracking. A project is a planned undertaking with a goal; it is something that exists in time with a distinct beginning and end.

Product management is about defining and marketing the things your company sells. It has nothing to do with the actual building of the product.

1. Write a specification.
2. Write the code.
3. Test the code against the specification.
4. Ship it!

This method is called *waterfall* based on the Gantt charts used to illustrate it, as in Figure 9, *Waterfall Gantt chart*, on page 185. (Real Gantt charts are often hundreds of tasks in size.) This method of project management collects all the tasks, time estimates for each task, and dependencies between tasks. Then it's a straightforward matter to lay them out and determine how long the whole project will take.

This style works well when the tasks are well-known and there isn't a lot of risk in the time estimates. In other fields of engineering, for example, building a road, the road engineers have a good idea of what they need to do and how long it takes. Likewise, if your team writes software to do customer billing and it already supports five methods of billing, adding another would be a project well-suited to waterfall management.

The key advantage of waterfall is its predictability: everyone has a shared understanding of what's to be done, how long it will take, and therefore how much it will cost.

Waterfall has a couple key vulnerabilities, too: first, when new invention is involved, it's impossible to tell at the outset of the project what tasks will be required or how long they'll take. Programmers must resort to guessing, and the compounded effect of hundreds of guesses is a huge wild-ass guess. *At best.*

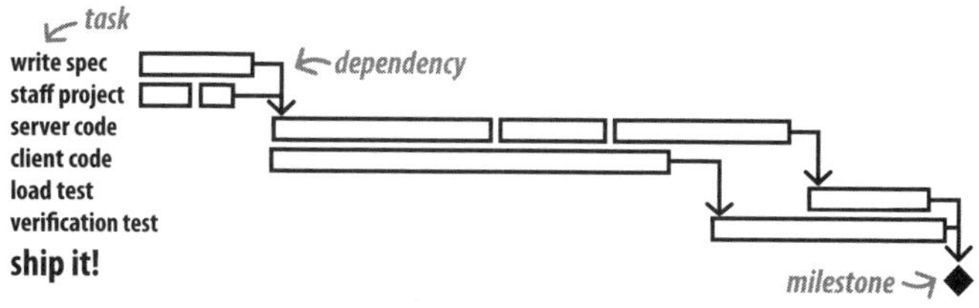

Figure 9—Waterfall Gantt chart

Second, waterfall leaves testing until the end. Technically, that testing is supposed to be a *verification* test, and there should be few surprises. It never works that way. In practice, engineering gets slack on quality—especially whole-system integration—because they assume the test phase will shake out the bugs. However, finding and fixing bugs becomes increasingly difficult as the software gets larger and worse when it's supposedly "done."

Your Role

In a waterfall project, you'll be given some chunk of the project requirements and then asked the following:

- What tasks does it take to meet the requirements?
- How long will each of them take?

The *totally honest* answer to both questions is, "I don't know." But your project manager won't take that one.

You'll have to take your best guess. Try to communicate the unknown factors as best you can. When almost everything is unknown, communicate *that*, too. I suggest doing this via email so you have a written record, in case someone later claims you didn't warn them of schedule risks.

When the schedule starts to fall apart—and it will—be sure to tell the project manager *as soon as you know* that a task is going to be late. The worst-case scenario for a six-month project is to be five months into it before the manager realizes there are another six months left to go. If you see the writing on the wall at month three, speak up, at least to your direct manager.

Agile Project Management

Programmers have questioned waterfall project management—a *defined process control* model—for years. In 2001 crystallized it with the Agile Manifesto,[1] which issued a clear challenge to reject our waterfall ways.

Agile is a form of *empirical process control*. The process is started with whatever data you have, and then it's measured while underway and adjusted based on those measurements. W. Edwards Deming applied this style of process control to manufacturing starting in the 1950s; his work was very influential to the Toyota Production System, the manufacturing process that Toyota used to become the world's largest automaker.

Agile starts with these assumptions:

- You can't specify anything more than about a month's worth of work, because you simply don't have enough information to do it accurately.

- The product requirements change often, so rather than resist that, just take it as a given.

- After-the-fact testing is wasteful; you should test from the beginning.

"Agile" is an over-arching term for this approach. There are many implementations: Scrum, Lean, and Extreme Programming,[2] for example. For a big-picture view, refer to *The Agile Samurai* [Ras10].

Central to agile is the concept of an iteration. This is simply a regular unit of time, with a single day as its smallest unit. Days are gathered into sprints (using Scrum parlance) of one to four weeks typically. Some number of sprints are needed to finish the features needed for a release. The iterations can be visualized like the nested circles of Figure 10, *Agile iterations*, on page 187.

---

1. http://agilemanifesto.org/
2. *Agile Project Management with Scrum* [Sch04]
    Lean Software Development: An Agile Toolkit for Software Development Managers [PP03]
    Extreme Programming Explained: Embrace Change [Bec00]

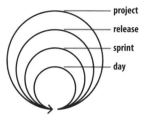

Figure 10—Agile iterations

Iterations in agile are opportunities for measurement and adaptation. A *daily stand-up* meeting is used to check in, across the team, each day. A *sprint review* is used to check in with stakeholders, and that's also the point where the sprint's software goals needs to be *done*. A goal may be very small in scope, but it should be production quality—the overall product should be potentially shippable to customers that very day.

It takes a lot of discipline across the whole team to get to a "done" that's production quality. Done includes development, integration, test, and documentation. The stakeholders may not *choose* to ship to customers at the end of a sprint—that's the larger topic of release planning—but part of the agreement in agile is that the product's quality never wavers.

Your Role

Working in an agile team is both demanding and rewarding. When you sign up for work, you'll still need to answer what tasks are needed and how long they'll take, but you're only answering for a small period of time (usually one to four weeks). At first you'll get it wrong, but you get quick feedback, so your ability to estimate will get better quickly.

When you consider your estimates, remember to include test time. Ideally your team uses automated tests, so that means more code you need to write. In my experience, there's about a 1:1 to 1:2 ratio between production code to automated test code. That means your optimistic thinking about the production code needs to be tempered by 100 percent to 200 percent to account for writing test code.

Finally, there's one sure thing about each agile iteration: when you finish one on Friday, there's another one starting next Monday. Sometimes you'll need to work long hours to meet your Friday commitment. Each time, however, learn from the experience and make better-educated estimates the next time. Long hours on a regular basis is a formula for burnout. Agile projects sustain an intense pace because you're held accountable to your commitments every couple weeks, so strive for working a solid forty hours but rarely more—those forty will be hard enough.

Actions

With this big-picture view of waterfall and agile, which style best matches your company? If it feels like some kind of hybrid—for example they use the term *sprints* but there's also a Gantt chart on the wall—then try to tease it apart by thinking in terms of *defined* vs. *empirical* process control.

Next, keep track of how accurately you estimate your work. You'll start by vastly underestimating. Use some empirical process control to improve: measure and adapt.

Finally, if you haven't met your project manager yet, go introduce yourself!

Tip 28

Appreciate the Circle of (a Product's) Life

[*Brown Belt*]   While you'll bury yourself in small-picture tasks at first, understanding the place of your project in the big-picture time-line will become important to your daily decision making.

Every product and service begins as a spark of inspiration in somebody's head. It's a long road between there and version 1.0, and longer still to version 10.0. This tip will take you on a tour of the life cycle for a product from a programmer's perspective.

The big-picture of a successful product is circular, as in Figure 11, *The product life cycle*, on page 190. Someone starts with a concept, builds prototypes, develops one into a product, and then releases it. It's a wild success, of course, and the company both maintains that product and starts developing new concepts. Eventually a product's time has passed, and it goes end-of-life; in the meantime, the company has built a stable of other successful products.

Not *every* product's life cycle is quite so complete; Silicon Valley is filled with the smoking craters of start-up companies that failed to get a product shipped or customers to buy. But we'll take the optimistic route and discuss a product with a long and healthy life.

Concept

In traditional product management, people research a market and look for opportunities. The *market* is short for *marketplace*; in practice, it's a definition of your customer. Who do you sell to? That's your market.

Opportunities, then, are products or services your customer is willing to pay for. At a market-driven company, they may do interviews, data mining, trend analysis, and other stuff

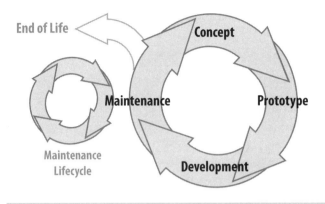

Figure 11—The product life cycle

that programmers generally find boring. Once they find a new opportunity for *ka-ching*, a product concept is born.

For dreamers and programmers, on the other hand, the concept phase goes the other way: a great product concept is born in someone's head; then they go looking for a market. This way is also known as "a solution looking for a problem." If there's a market for the product, there's nothing wrong with this technique—in fact, it's the way many disruptive technologies get created.

Your Role

Let's say you have some cred and you've been invited to join a team in the concept phase. What do the programmers do when there's nothing yet to program? Eat pizza and drink beer while the marketing department figures things out?

I can't argue with the pizza or beer part—take that if you can get it. But to earn your keep in this phase, you need to be evaluating each concept and figuring out what's actually possible, lest marketing dream up something that would require a quantum computer to actually build.

You can contribute concepts, too. The technology world is constantly changing, and new concepts become possible as a result. For example, as computers have advanced in speed, more and more has become possible in gaming industry graphics. Text-based games gave way to iconic 2D graphics. Static graphics gave way to dynamically rendered graphics.

Waterfall vs. Agile Terminology

Our discussion here is about the *product* life cycle, which is different from the *project* life cycle discussed in Tip 27, *Get with the Project*, on page 183. With waterfall-style development, the distinction is academic; there's one project whose purpose is to build the product.

In agile development, there's an continuous cycle of iterations that are smaller, fixed-length projects. What we're discussing in this tip is a *release* rather than a project. Release planning is done by the product owner.

2D gave way to 3D...each of these revolutions in gaming started with some programmer saying, "Hey, now that we have [x], I bet we could use that to do [y]."

Driving Spikes

Another important job in concept stage is what we call *driving spikes*. It's a form of research where you go deep but narrow, usually for the purpose of evaluating a new technology or possibility. Say you've read about threaded network IO vs. event-driven IO, and you want to know which would be best for your web application. The only way to find out is to try.

Driving a spike is different from academic research, because you're not trying to become an expert in the field; you're trying to answer a specific question. It's not the same as prototyping, because you're not building a whole product mock-up, just a small piece.

You may need to drive a spike at any time in the product life cycle, but the concept phase in particular is where you have a world of options open to you, and it's your job to figure out which are feasible and which are not. It's also possible you'll discover something unexpected and create a new concept from it.

Finally, when you're new and have a lot to learn, driving spikes is a great way to get some experience. Say you've read about threaded vs. event-driven network IO, but you haven't written *any* networking programs before. While the rest of the team is evaluating product concepts, ask your manager for some time to drive a spike on networking. Then bust out the books and get busy.

Prototype

A concept may look great on paper, but a working prototype is where it comes to life. The purpose of the prototype phase is twofold: first, it's to teach prospective customers (and your company's stakeholders) what the product will do. This is great for getting market feedback, promoting the product ahead of its release, and showing your financiers that you're doing something useful with their money.

The second purpose is learning how to build the *real* product. It's a fact of life that you always get some stuff wrong the first time around; the prototypes are where you get to crash and burn and then try again. Fortunately, in our industry, the "crash and burn" part is *usually* only figurative. (I've worked on hardware projects where it was literal.)

Sometimes products get killed at the prototype phase because, with prototype in hand, it becomes clear that the product isn't compelling to the customer. It's better to learn these things sooner than later; assuming your company wasn't founded on this one product concept, you move onto the next concept and start again.

Your Role

Now you definitely have to work to earn your pizza. Prototypes need programming, with an emphasis on covering a lot of ground fast. When you're junior, you'll probably be working under a tech lead who is responsible for the overall design of the prototype, but the lead will need help filling in all the gaps. The prototype may be the digital equivalent of cardboard and duct tape, but when the job requires a *whole lot* of duct tape, junior engineers are often selected to help.

The best thing you can do is shadow the tech lead or architect—get the cube next to him, ask to move into his office, whatever it takes to be right there. Your goal in prototype phase is to bang out something quick, and that requires constant communication with the rest of the team, especially the lead.

Development

After the prototypes are made and the executives have confidence that the product concept has some meat to it, it's time to start building the real thing. This is where the project staffs up, where plans and schedules are established, and where you get down to the business of "real" programming. You'll spend much of your career in this stage.

While prototype programming and development programming both boil down to programming, there's a critical shift in mind-set. Your goals are longer-term, and shortcuts are guaranteed to bite you in the ass later. This is code that's *going to ship to paying customers*, and they have assumptions about product quality: it can't suck.

Quality is a big enough topic that we cover it separately in Chapter 1, *Program for Production*, on page 3. Likewise, the processes used to manage development are covered in Tip 27, *Get with the Project*, on page 183.

Your Role

Now you have a pretty clear picture of what you need to do, so it's time to execute. We often speak of programming as a craft and creative work, but you also have to deliver what's required for the product. If you're told to write the installer, for example, it's not going to require tremendous creativity. To the contrary, that's a pretty standardized task, and "creative" solutions will get you into more trouble than following established conventions.

Where established best practices exist, *follow them* unless you really have a compelling reason not to (and I mean *really* compelling). At the beginning, you won't know where best practices exist and where they don't, so think of it this way: is your task something that has probably been done a thousand times before?

Installer programs? Check, been done before.

In cases like this, go find a book—the company will pay for it. Really, there's no point in reinventing the wheel, not on a commercial product. This mistake is common enough that it has its own name: not invented here syndrome (NIHS). I was at a company that invented a novel user interface for

Real Artists Ship

A Steve Jobs mantra during the development of the Macintosh was "real artists ship."[a] The creators of the Macintosh had the not-so-humble goal of making a dent in the universe, but they knew that you couldn't make a dent if you didn't get the product out the door.

Programmers are always tempted to add one more feature or fix one more bug. We don't want to let the product out the door because we keep thinking of ways to make it better. Management, on the other hand, always wants to ship one day sooner. Who's right?

Both viewpoints make the product better. It's a maxim of the technology world that version 1.1 of any product is what version 1.0 should have been. That's true because *real-world feedback* to 1.0 drives the improvements in 1.1. There's no shortcut; you have to ship 1.0—warts and all—and let customers tell you what 1.1 should be.

---

a.   http://c2.com/cgi/wiki?RealArtistsShip

mobile computing (a worthy pursuit), but we *also* invented our own operating system, our own networking protocols, our own network, our own silicon to run everything on...the result? A $200-million crater in the middle of Silicon Valley.

Instead of NIHS, focus your creativity on where your program is *different* from the other stuff out there. Ask your manager or peers: what's novel about what we're doing? That's where creativity pays off. As the new person, you may not be assigned to work on the creative stuff—the senior engineers have called dibs on that—but you can still play with ideas and take some time to experiment. That's showing initiative, and most teams reward it.

For all tasks, novel or not, craftsmanship still plays a central role. When you're plodding through the installer program, following established conventions and not getting fancy, you still have to *get it right*. That means paying careful attention to detail, thorough testing, proper integration with your company's release control process, and so forth. Use the project as an opportunity to build cred as a solid engineer.

Release

Project managers have a saying: the software is done when you rip it out of the programmer's hands. Your team will never be fully *ready* for release, but at some point management decides they're done waiting, so they rip it out of your team's hands and ship it. Have a party, drink a beer—you've earned it!

While a product release might seem like a one-day event, it's actually a huge logistical challenge for the entire company: manufacturing (for hardware) gets their line going, the deployment team (for websites) stages the rollout of the site, marketing does a big push to get the message out, sales starts booking orders, support responds to customer problems, and so forth.

While that's going on, you'll have enough work within engineering to keep you plenty busy. Your team will have a release process that goes something like this:

1. (Before release) The build master or tech lead will use the version control system to create a "stable" release branch separate from the mainline code. There will be some policy on the release branch to control changes, usually requiring code review and sign-off from the tech lead.

2. When the team thinks the release branch is ready, it's tagged as a *release candidate,* and someone does an official RC build. This gets unique version number, something like "1.0-RC1."

3. The test department and possibly external beta testers beat on RC1 and flush out bugs.

4. (Repeat these steps until management calls it done.)

5. The final release candidate gets one final change in source control; the version number becomes 1.0, and someone does the gold master build.

6. Ship it!

For web companies, the process is a bit more fluid, but the same principles apply: branch the code to control changes, test the snot out of the branch, and then push the code to the public-facing servers.

The final step is both a "we're done" and a "we're just beginning" moment at the same time. Yes, version 1.0 was called done and shipped. But as soon as the first customer starts using the product, you start to respond to problems. (You probably know of some looming problems already—no product ships completely bug-free.) Congratulate yourself on the "we're done" part, but don't be surprised, or discouraged, when a day later it shifts to "we're just beginning."

Your Role

This varies depending on the kind of product and the size of your company. In a small hardware company, you could get recruited to help build the first batch of products. (I've been there, actually soldering boards to fill a big order.) In a web company, you may be on the hook to babysit some of the servers, update their code, and watch to see whether they barf.

I've never worked in a company where the release was a "throw it over the wall" moment where everything was just *done* and I could slack. As a junior guy, I was on the hook to help support the rollout. As a senior guy, I'm on the hook to go to trade shows and key customers to promote the release.

To that end, you won't need to look for where to help with the release; it'll be obvious. Help where you can and figure on some long hours. Consider it a bonding experience with the team.

Maintenance

Up to now we've been talking about the product life cycle leading to initial release. However, if a product drives a healthy business, you don't just ship 1.0 and call it done. Customer demand fuels ongoing development of new versions of the product. For example, Microsoft Windows 1.0 was released in 1985, but it's a product that has evolved greatly over time. If Microsoft has its way, Windows will *never* be done.

At this point the development cycle branches: part of the company goes back to concept phase to develop the next version of the product; another part takes care of the existing customers. The latter part is maintenance phase. This is a common job for junior programmers.

Maintenance takes various forms depending on the kind of product you make. For hardware this includes support and repair. It can also include feature-neutral product development, either for cost reduction or because upstream parts are no longer available. CPUs, for example, have a very short life cycle, so hardware with embedded CPUs often needs to be revised to use newer parts.

For software there are bug fixes and updates for compatibility. If you sell a Windows application and Microsoft releases a new version of Windows, you may need to update your software. Websites have the same issues—new versions of web browsers come out constantly. Added to this, most software products make use of upstream vendors, for example for payment processing or server hosting.

A common complaint is "You have to run just to stay in the same place." It can be frustrating trying to keep pace with the world changing around you—especially when you're trying to keep customers happy *and* build the next version of the product at the same time.

The Maintenance Life Cycle

The maintenance phase looks like its own mini life cycle: you start from a concept, maybe build prototypes, develop and test, and then release. The only real difference between the maintenance phase and new product development is the "new" part. Some maintenance efforts can include enough features that the line gets very blurry indeed.

Your role doesn't change much either way: you're still building a product and releasing it to the world. In some ways, incremental releases can be easier than 1.0 because they're smaller in scope. In other ways, they can be harder because real customers have your product and you can't break something that is working for them today.

Your Role

Maintenance is a common training ground for new hires. There's usually less time pressure to get to the next release, plus the senior engineers have already called dibs on whatever new project is spinning up. Thus, you get to maintain the existing product.

Unlike the Maytag repairman, there's *always* stuff to do on software. Version 1.0 didn't ship because it was perfect; to the contrary, it shipped with a ton of bugs that your customers are probably already raising a ruckus about. Most likely, your primary responsibility will be bug patrol.

This is an opportunity to get to know the software and prove you can work on it effectively. As you fix problems, document the following in the bug-tracking system or version control system:

- The bug should already contain detailed observations about the problem. Elaborate in the problem description if needed.

- Analysis of the problem; explain the root cause if possible. Sometimes this can't be determined conclusively. Do your best to explain your hypothesis and supporting evidence.

- Explanation of your fix. This should include an overview of code changes and any effects users might observe.

- How to test your changes.

This is simply the scientific method as applied to software. Deliver on these points, and you'll quickly earn a reputation for solid thinking and programming.

End of Life

Sometimes a product is just "done." This could happen for any number of reasons: the company goes belly-up, the product is not profitable, the company replaces a product with a new product, and so forth. This is a strategy-level decision, which you may contribute to later in your career, but for now it's merely informational.

For hardware, EOL is a fact of life; no hardware product stays relevant for very long. For example, when Intel makes a CPU, there's little guarantee you'll be able to buy the same CPU a year later—competition forces them to constantly move on.

Software is a little fuzzier; usually software *versions* go EOL but the software product as a whole continues with new versions. Websites are the ultimate extension of this. They continuously roll new versions, and unless the front end changes, the user isn't even aware of it.

Your Role

The EOL decision belongs to the executives—you'll just come into work one day and find out you're on a new project. (Or out of a job, in the unhappy case where the company goes belly-up.)

However, programmers aren't always off the hook at EOL. Your team may be tasked with helping the customer transition to the next generation of products. For example, Apple set an excellent example with CPU transitions: in the 1990s it switched CPUs from Motorola 68K to PowerPC, a completely different architecture. However, Apple included an emulator that allowed customers to run their existing 68K applications on PowerPC, thus giving their users several years to upgrade their software. Apple did the same thing in the 2000s, switching from PowerPC to Intel x86. Apple *programmed* the customer's pain out of migrating to new hardware.

Actions

Now that you have a big-picture map, it's time to figure out where your product is at. Talk with your manager—or even better, the product manager—about where they see the product in its life cycle. Also, review the appropriate *your role* section in this tip.

That established, where's the product going next? And in what kind of timeframe? This question is best addressed to the product manager; if you don't know that person yet, refer to *Product Management*, on page 167.

Tip 29

Put Yourself in the Company's Shoes

 [*Black Belt*]   Once in a while, you'll want to mentally check in with the company's big-picture goals. Do you understand *why* and *where* it's going?

Let's say you've joined a company that's setting out to change the world. When your product ships, it'll revolutionize the way people communicate, keep track of their kids, and do their laundry. That's fine and good, but your product is not the underlying reason the company exists.

"Why are we here?" is perhaps the biggest of big-picture questions. Its answer, however, is simple: the role, the underlying *raison d'être*, of any company is to *protect the investment and interests of its shareholders*.

You may think, "Am I merely the tool of greedy capitalist investors?" Well, most likely, to a degree...*yes*. But before pledging your undying allegiance to Richard Stallman and free software, let's back up and consider that the role stated earlier is true even for altruistic organizations.

Take a nonprofit organization like One Laptop Per Child (OLPC), whose mission is "to create educational opportunities for the world's poorest children by providing each child with a rugged, low-cost, low-power, connected laptop with content and software designed for collaborative, joyful, self-empowered learning."[4]

For shareholders in OLPC, they've put in money, time, and/or expertise. Protecting their investment means keeping OLPC afloat—OLPC needs to keep bringing in money so they can keep pumping out laptops. Protecting the shareholder's interests means keeping OLPC true to the cause. The kids need laptops for learning; that's what OLPC

---

4.   http://laptop.org/en/vision/index.shtml

shareholders signed up for, so the organization can't switch to One Toaster Per Child (even if the toaster runs NetBSD).

Now with a more-profit-the-better company, the role can be simplified to: *ka-ching! ka-ching! ka-ching!* The investors may not care if they're investing in technology or investing in soap, so long as they get some ROI. Now we're talking callous: is money *your* ultimate goal? If not, how do your interests match up with the shareholders?

Let's say you're truly the tool of greedy capitalists; you program so they can profit. There's another side to the deal: they're paying your salary. They've taken a risk by paying you good money so you can go program and *maybe* the resulting product or service will pan out.

Frankly, this can be a perfectly good deal. If you're building the right product the right way and the rest of the business works out as planned, you get your satisfaction and the shareholders get their money. Everyone wins. And if the business doesn't work out, it turns out you get to keep the money they paid you anyway. Both you and the shareholders move onto the next job.

Actions

Let's try to bring some of this abstract stuff closer to home. For this exercise, you may need help from your manager.

Let's pick apart the statement that a company's purpose is to protect the investment and interests of its shareholders:

- Shareholders: who are they? If your company is publicly traded, they're obvious: anyone who owns stock. Can you pick that apart any further and find out who has most of the stock? (This may take some research.) If your company is private, it still has stock; the difference is that its stock is not traded in an open market. The bulk of the stock is usually owned by the founders, angel investors, and/or venture capitalists.

- Investment and interests: Now that you know *who* the shareholders are, can you figure out what it means to protect their investment and interests? The *investment* part is obvious—don't waste their money. The *interest*

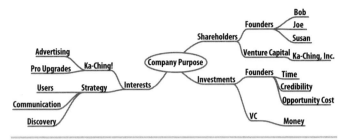

Figure 12—Fictional company's purpose

part can be more complicated. (With a venture capitalist, it's easy: *ka-ching!*)

A more complex case could be a partner company; their interest in your success may indirectly benefit another part of their business. For example, CPU maker AMD was an early sponsor of the One Laptop Per Child project. This was partly so OLPC would use AMD chips *(ka-ching!)* but also for the more strategic purpose of establishing AMD's brand in developing countries.

- Connect the dots: here's where the rubber meets the road. Can you connect the dots from the shareholders and their interests to the product you're making? Or to put it another way, how will the success of your product protect the investment and interests of the company's shareholders?

Figure 12, *Fictional company's purpose*, on page 202 is a mind map for an imaginary company founded by a couple people (Bob, Joe, Susan) and funded by a venture capital firm. They're doing a social networking website (isn't everybody?) that they hope will make money from advertising and premium subscriptions.

In your map you could follow each branch a few more levels down. (To learn more about mind mapping as a tool for generating ideas and associations, see *Pragmatic Thinking and Learning* [Hun08].)

Tip 30

Identify Corporate Antipatterns

 [*White Belt*] Keep a watchful eye for stupidity—it could strike at any moment.

You may have heard of programming *design patterns*, where people have identified recurring patterns of programming solutions that have proven useful. This section is the opposite, a collection of recurring patterns of business practices that have often proven counterproductive, misinformed, or downright stupid.

You won't be able to fix these yourself; problems at this scale can take years and many hands to build. I document these as a warning, in the same way that wilderness survival guides include pictures of poisonous plants.

Will any of this business buffoonery kill you? No, but it foretells rough times ahead. If you hear "The schedule is king," your project is heading for a death march. The *hockey stick sales curve* is often followed by flat sales.

So, take note, and be prepared for a new job search if your company turns poisonous.

The Schedule Is King

Project managers love Gantt charts. Remember the simple one from *Waterfall Project Management*, on page 183? Imagine that with 500 lines and 100 cross-dependencies. That's the kind of Gantt charts project managers actually make.

Then management buys off on the intricate schedule that says the product will ship in eighteen months. But there's a catch: the product really has to ship in eighteen months. After all, there's this scientific-looking graph *proving* it can ship in eighteen months, right? The rallying cry is, "The schedule is king."

Nobody can predict a complex project eighteen months out. The intricate Gantt chart is based on wild guesses and assumptions that couldn't possibly be validated. The schedule falls apart within months.

However, management sticks doggedly to the schedule—after all, *the schedule is king*. Throw out features, throw out testing, throw out whatever it takes to ship *something* on the scheduled end date. Then leave it to the beleaguered sales and marketing teams to figure out how to put lipstick on the pig.

What do you do when faced with "the schedule is king"? I would *not* recommend telling management which bodily orifice you think they pulled the schedule out of. Instead, be honest to management when scheduled tasks take longer than expected (they will) or quality is slipping (it will). Don't say "I told you so"—just stick to the facts. A good manager will take the facts back to the rest of the company and figure out where to go from there.

Furthermore, when it comes time to cut features (and it will), then don't immediately suggest cutting the features that are hard to implement. As much as possible, think about the product *as a customer* and what features you'd really want. Some of them will be hard. Regardless, stick up for the features in proportion to the value they'd give the customer.

The Mythical Man-Month

The Mythical Man-Month [Bro95] by Fred Brooks is a famous book in the high-tech world. It seems like everyone has read it. It seems like everyone has forgotten it, too.

The premise is that management sees a schedule slipping, and since the schedule is king, they decide to add more programmers to the project. If it takes five programmers ten months to develop the product, shouldn't it take ten programmers five months? Fred Brooks, however, asserts that adding programmers to a late project *makes the project later*.

The problem is that programming in a team requires a great deal of communication and coordination. Managers will lament that it's like herding cats. It's not that programmers are stupid or dysfunctional; it's just the nature of creating complex systems. Pile more people in the room, and now you have a complex system *and* a complex coordination problem on your hands.

What do you do when faced with management adding a bunch of programmers to your project? Honestly, you won't get much say in the matter. The very best thing you can do, however, is *talk frequently* with your other team members. When possible, get people chatting around a whiteboard. Or pair up with someone when writing complex code. However you can do it, keep communication channels open. This will benefit the project but also establish *you* as a person who knows what's going on.

The Hockey Stick Sales Curve

This one is my favorite, because I actually heard it at General Magic, and it was later immortalized in a Dilbert cartoon. The guy puts up a chart like Figure 13, *Don't believe the hockey stick*, on page 206 and begins his pitch:

> We expect the adoption rate to be slow for the first couple quarters, but then the product's popularity reaches a critical mass and sales take off, like a hockey stick!

Yea, right. The hockey stick does indeed happen for some companies, but a company can't make that hockey stick happen through wishful thinking. Ultimately, the market needs to drive it. The company can't predict if or when that will even happen. Great products sometimes wither and die; mediocre products can take off. Who knows which will hockey stick and which won't?

An honest business case may include the hockey stick as a best-case scenario, but it will also include the reality-check scenario where the product doesn't go gangbusters all of a sudden.

What do you do when faced with the hockey stick presentation? That depends. In my case, I was having a great time and the company was still flush with cash, so who cares? I kept on programming. But if your company is small, product sales are needed to pay your paycheck and you get this pitch…start thinking about other jobs.

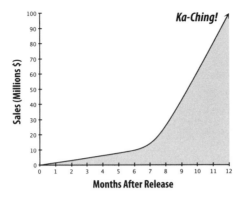

Figure 13—Don't believe the hockey stick

The Big Rewrite

Programmers mired in legacy code often wish they could throw it all away and start over. Once in a while, they convince the stakeholders that it's the right thing to do.

The Big Rewrite ensues. Programmers hold lots of design meetings. New technologies are chosen. Things are really fun because the sky is the limit on the new code base.

Then things get hard: it turns out that a lot of that gnarly code in the previous product was actually needed for something. All that nasty GUI setup code was needed by an old version of Windows, and your biggest customer still runs that version of Windows. All the special cases in the workflow code is there because those special cases are intrinsic to the problem domain. Oh no...the new version is becoming legacy, and it hasn't even shipped yet!

Making problems worse, nobody figured on all this extra work up front. When the stakeholders agreed to the Big Rewrite, they thought it would take six months. Now the team is six months in but not halfway done yet. Not-too-kind questions are being asked by management. Your work hours get longer. And in everyone's haste to finish, quality goes down the drain. Things are really *not fun* anymore.

What do you do in the face of a big rewrite? First, read Tip 7, *Improve Legacy Code*, on page 48. There are techniques for dealing with legacy code that don't involve throwing every-thing out and starting over.

Second, refer to Tip 4, *Tame Complexity*, on page 27, with a special emphasis on separating necessary complexity from accidental complexity. You can't throw out the necessary complexity. But ask the team: are there ways you can model it better?

Actions

As mentioned up front, by the time you spot one of these business-level antipatterns, it's probably too late, and a lone programmer wouldn't be able to fix it anyway. So, I leave you with one action: when your peers begin jumping ship, ask them, "Are there any more jobs open at *that* company?"

Part IV

Looking Forward

CHAPTER 7

Kaizen

Kaizen is a Japanese term for continuous improvement. No matter your level of programming mastery, you can always do better. Obvious, perhaps, but I've met programmers who appeared to peak about five to ten years into their career and then…just stick there.

Continuous improvement and mastery of our trade takes some obvious forms: learning a new programming language, broadening your skills in a new area of computing, or building your chops by contributing to an open source project. These are all great ways to challenge yourself and keep fresh. However, think of kaizen in broader terms.

By *mastery*, I'm not just referring to technologies. There are programmers who mastered C decades ago and have been writing system software ever since. Are they stagnant? Not necessarily — we continue to see tremendous feats of engineering in operating systems. C itself may not be new and shiny, but it's still a foundational language used to build new and shiny stuff.

Further, by *improvement*, I don't just mean learning things at an intellectual level. Your attitude toward your work dramatically affects your productivity and the quality of the code you write. Your interactions with other people likewise affect your professional development and ability to deliver products. These are areas you can improve, even though they deal with the messy, irrational, and emotional aspects of life.

In our final section of the book, we look forward. You're already improving—kaizen is about keeping that ball rolling.

- We start on a tip with attitude: Tip 31, *Mind Your Head*, on page 213 argues the "glass half-full" point of view. You may choose the "Glass is twice as large as it needs to be" perspective if you prefer.

- Just when you thought you could take a break from the books, Tip 32, *Never Stop Learning*, on page 217 looks at ways to continue honing your skills.

- Tip 33, *Find Your Place*, on page 222 closes our book with some future opportunities for the career programmer.

Tip 31

Mind Your Head

 [*White Belt*] Your attitude affects both your productivity and your future all day, every day.

In the 1990s Bare Bones Software released a text editor called BBEdit with the tagline "It Doesn't Suck." It retains the tagline to this day. Truly brilliant marketing. Who's their market? Programmers.

Programmers are a pessimistic and sarcastic lot. The vast majority will tell you about 100 things that suck for every one thing that doesn't. The highest praise a programmer will give a product is, "It doesn't suck."

Pessimist programmers are in good company. I've read various reports saying the vast majority of projects fail,[1] 80 or 90 percent. Adding insult to injury, it's not the good 10 or 20 percent that succeed; it's some hodgepodge of good and bad. It almost seems that bland to downright crappy products are more successful, on average, than really good ones. When a programmer says such-and-such sucks, chances are she's right.

The gambler would simply say everything sucks—playing those odds isn't rocket science. But here's the problem: you don't win anything for picking losers.

Balancing the Odds

When I was an industry newbie, my first manager told me, "Being a pessimist is the easiest thing in the world. It's the easy way out. It's much harder to be an optimist." Those

---

1. The most common source is the Standish Group's CHAOS Report, http://www.standishgroup.com/. However, there are numerous challengers of the CHAOS report, e.g., http://doi.acm.org/10.1145/1145287.1145301 and http://dx.doi.org/10.1109/MS.2009.154 and others.

words—and that challenge—changed my tone and my career.

When you shift your perspective from "It sucks" to "Wouldn't it be cool if…," you shift from a defeatist mind-set to a creative mind-set. The best you can do from a *sucks* attitude is create something that sucks slightly less. From a *cool* attitude, you can create something completely new.

Creating new things is a practiced skill. Starting from school, you've been trained to follow examples and create small bits of new work. With practice, you'll create larger works and also deviate further from prior examples into work wholly of your own imagination.

Your rate of learning is largely determined by how much you want to push yourself, and that push comes from your attitude.

Structure for Creation

Robert Fritz, in his book *The Path of Least Resistance* [Fri89], identifies two *structures* for how we interact with our world.

Reactive/Responsive

This is our default structure, where we react to circumstances. To a programmer, this could go something like this: you want to reduce the number of bugs in the product (responding to testers), and likewise you want to get the product out the door (responding to management pressure). Pulled between these forces—forces pulling in opposite directions—you make fixes that are good enough to fix the bugs without jeopardizing the schedule.

This is also known as *fire-fighting mode*. You may put out the fire today, but you never get around to addressing systematic, big-picture problems in the product.

Creative

Rather than immediately responding to present circumstances, in the creative mode you acknowledge the present state and visualize a better future state. For example, you visualize a product that is more modular and therefore easier to test and reason about. Guided by this creative vision, you go into the code looking for opportunities to make it modular as you're fixing the bugs. (See Tip 7, *Improve Legacy Code*, on page 48 for some advice on *finding seams* in legacy code.)

What's the difference? In the long run, the reactive/responsive bug fixing will leave you with a code base that's even more gnarly to maintain than when you started. The *hard* bugs will just be patched over, not really fixed. In the creative structure, on the other hand, you have a guiding vision that will improve the code base—including the hard bits—over time.

Creating a vision engenders—in fact, it *requires*—a positive attitude. You can't create anything out of pessimism. It also requires hard work to bring that creative vision into reality, but the work is no harder than you'd be doing anyway. The bonus is that when you're driving toward a vision of a better future, the hard work is fulfilling in a way that you don't get from reactive work.

Evangelism

The next level of creative vision is bringing others along for the ride. Early in your career, you may be on the receiving end of technology evangelism. I would hope so, because it's tremendously fun to *believe* in what you're doing. Later, you'll create and evangelize on your own.

Evangelism is tremendously underrated in the technology world. People think of computers as, well, boring machines, so what's there to get excited about? But think about your early, wide-eyed play with computers: didn't you dive in with vigor and passion? Of course…that's why you're here today, reading this book.

An evangelist reignites that passion and directs it to a vision of something new and cool. (It may be a vision that would be profitable once created, but the focus of evangelism is more about the spirit than the dollars.) This isn't just the job of CEOs and marketing folks; programmers can be just as talented at evangelism as anyone. It's that conversation that starts with "Wouldn't it be cool if…,"

There's absolutely nothing deceitful about evangelism; it's just painting a picture of a better future state so that others can understand it and believe in it. Terence Ryan's *Driving Technical Change* [Rya10] is a great resource for learning this skill. Guy Kawasaki, one of Apple's early evangelists, gives a big-picture view of evangelism in his book *Selling the Dream* [Kaw92].

Now "It Doesn't Suck" doesn't seem like such a brilliant product tagline after all. (To its credit, it still makes me laugh.) Think hard about the reputation you want to establish. Visualize—yes, create—in your mind the *you* five years from now. Are you the naysayer, or are you the one inspiring people to make something cool?

Actions

Think about your most inspiring teacher (in school or otherwise). What was it about them that made them so great? Write in your journal characteristics of how they talked about their subject and how that inspired you to think about the subject.

Watch some recorded presentations of great product announcements, for example Steve Jobs introducing the Macintosh. Observe how the presenter doesn't sell the product so much as the *vision* of the product—the *dream* behind the product. That's evangelism at work.

Tip 32

Never Stop Learning

 *[Brown Belt]* You already have a ton to learn on the job; focus on those near-term needs first. However, don't put off sharpening your skills for long—they'll get dull faster than you think.

You might puzzle over the title of this tip, thinking "I'll always keep on learning." However, it's easy to lose this in the shuffle. The job gets busy, you have family and hobbies after work, and next thing you know it's been five years since you put effort into learning a new skill.

It's up to you to keep learning. Do it on company time, do it on your own time, or do whatever it takes to keep fresh. Part of the goal is to keep yourself marketable in an ever-changing industry, but an even larger part is to keep up your ability to learn.

Learn How You're Wired

The *right* way to learn varies from person to person; some learn best by reading books, others do well in the classroom, and still others need to get hands-on. If you struggled in school, consider that the way they taught may not match the way you naturally learn.

You owe it to yourself to pick up a copy of Andy Hunt's *Pragmatic Thinking and Learning* [Hun08] to discover your optimal learning style. Unlike the force-feeding nature of school, *this* learning is driven by *you* so you can do it in the style that suits you.

If you don't already know your learning style, consider a personality test like Myers-Briggs (described in Tip 21, *Grok Personality Types*, on page 135). There are also less-formal surveys floating around the Internet. Or, simply take the empirical approach: grab a book, download some podcasts, find a video or screencast. Which one do you gravitate to?

Keep Current

It's said (a bit too often, admittedly) that "You need to run just to stand still" in the technology world. It's true. If you get cozy in a job and stop keeping abreast of new developments, your next job hunt could prove very difficult. It makes sense to dedicate time to exploring new technologies simply for risk mitigation.

Since you can't keep abreast of *everything*, how do you prioritize? On the one hand, you want to track new technologies while they're still trending up. On the other hand, some fads come and go without making a dent in industry. So you want to find technologies that have reached a *tipping point*[2] of critical mass.

My personal bellwether is watching recently published books—the paper kind—since publishers are looking for the same sweet spot. They want to keep their books on the leading edge but need a large enough audience to offset the cost of making a book. Blogs aren't as reliable because you'll always find *someone* who will blog about *anything*, making it hard to tell the difference between critical mass and passing fads. Job listings follow much too late, because they're usually written by managers who don't keep close tabs on technology.

Broaden Your Thinking

Where *keeping current* is mostly about risk mitigation, there's also tremendous merit—and fun—to learning technologies that have *nothing* to do with economic interests. Sometimes you should step out of the world of commercial tech and flex your brain muscles.

Do a gut-feel check: are there things you're curious about but never spent the time to research? Maybe it's Scheme. Or microcontrollers. Or even learning a new text editor. Make a weekend project out of one of these and dive into it. If

---

2. For a complete discussion, see *The Tipping Point* [Gla02] by Malcolm Gladwell.

> ## Industry Perspective: You Can't Get Better Without Practice
>
> Coding is like playing guitar: you have to do it to learn it. The more you do it, the better you get. You can't just read books and become a better coder. There's absolutely no shortcuts, so if you don't *enjoy* coding right now, you probably won't get good at it later.
>
> *–Scott "Zz" Zimmerman, senior software engineer*

you've been brought up on C++ and Java, I assure you that diving into Scheme with *Structure and Interpretation of Computer Programs* [AS96] will make your head spin.

The real magic is that digging into Scheme with SICP won't just make you a better Scheme programmer. Forcing yourself out of your comfort zone and reasoning about code in a different manner will improve your ability to reason about *all* code, not just Scheme.

Community

School provides a tremendous support structure for students. It has your peers, professors, and a huge library to help back you up. Your day job, on the other hand, is geared toward *shipping it*. It's up to you to build the support structure you need for learning.

Look around at your programmer friends. Do any of them have the same learning style as you? If you're a reader, form a book club. Visual learners can have a lot of fun problem solving at the whiteboard. Auditory learners need to talk and listen, which is a lot more fun when you have someone to talk to.

Next, cast your net wider. Most technologies have some combination of blogs, forums, news groups, IRC channels, and user groups. Where available, an in-person user group often has the best signal-to-noise ratio. Websites like MeetUp[3] can help you find a local user's group.

---

3.   http://www.meetup.com/

Then you need some motivation. Open source projects are a great way to give purpose to your learning. You obviously can't jump into a project without building up some skill, but even at junior skill levels you can find ways to contribute, for example by writing documentation. By working in the open, you build ad hoc peer groups that keep you engaged and active.

You can find tons of open source projects on websites like GitHub[4] and SourceForge.[5] Many programming languages also have directories of projects written in that language, for example RubyForge[6] for Ruby projects.

Conferences

Technology conferences range from expensive weeklong affairs in exotic vacation spots to one-day freebies at a local hotel. (Your company will occasionally pay for an expensive one.) These are great opportunities for learning and meeting programmers from other companies.

Many conferences have multiple *tracks* with sessions of a similar theme. Pick a track or just cherry-pick the sessions that look interesting. All conferences also have an additional track—the *hallway track*. That's all the interesting stuff you learn just by chatting with folks in the hallway between sessions. Often the hallway track is more interesting than anything else at the conference.

(Keep in mind that conferences are partly for your benefit but largely for the benefit of the vendors sponsoring the thing. The email address you use to register for the conference will *forever* be a target for vendors' promotional emails.)

Bill the Company

While learning is primarily for your benefit, don't forget that your current employer has some self-interest, too. As you learn new skills, the company is getting a more skilled programmer. Thus, they'll often foot the bill. Books, classes, and conferences are all fair game—ask your manager.

---

4.   http://github.com
5.   http://sourceforge.net
6.   http://rubyforge.org

Many managers, in fact, have an ongoing task to send their employees to training. Much like your own learning, it's easy for this to get lost in the shuffle. Therefore, when *you* take the reins, you do your manager a favor as well as yourself.

Actions

Make a mind map of the skills you have right now: programming languages, platforms, tools, and so forth. Some of your map's branches will look sparse. Identify a couple areas where you're lacking—and you're motivated to improve—and commit to improving them over the next six months.

Set aside some money each month as a self-improvement fund. This could be for books, software, or other resources you need. (Beer does not count as a self-improvement resource.) Then you won't need to worry about shelling out some cash when you have time to pick up something new. You have the money ready to go.

Research a programming language that is as *different* as possible from the language you use at your day job. For C++ (statically typed, compiled, object-oriented), this might be Scheme (dynamically typed, interpreted, functional); for Ruby, it might be Haskell. Buy a book or two (Bruce Tate's *Seven Languages in Seven Weeks* [Tat10], for example), dedicate some time, and flex those brain muscles.

Tip 33

Find Your Place

[*Black Belt*]   This topic looks far into the future. Don't worry about it yet—but don't ignore it forever, either.

At this point, you're getting your footing in the industry. Figure on five to ten years of building experience and credibility. What lies past that for a programmer? I mean, aside from obscene wealth, a big house, and a fast car?

Programming to...Programming

First of all, there's programming. For some, that's what you're put on Earth to do, and you can make a good living doing it, so why stop? Many companies have acknowledged the value of very skilled programmers, and your pay can keep climbing—you don't need to go into management to get the bucks.

However, some companies are not so progressive. If you stay in programming more than ten years, you'll need to shop around more for jobs. I've talked to a number of tech companies whose pay simply tops out no matter how good you are, and I've talked with managers who won't pay a programmer more than the manager makes. There's no use in trying to convince them otherwise; just move along.

Another option is contracting. You bid on jobs either by the hour or by completion of the job. The upside is you (usually) make a lot more money per hour. The downside is you need to look for jobs a lot more often—and in lean times you may not be able to find any. Before considering this route, you must have a sufficient professional network for finding jobs, plus enough money in the bank to sustain your household when a job falls through.

The best resource for advancing your programming career is Chad Fowler's *The Passionate Programmer: Creating a*

Remarkable Career in Software Development [Fow09]. He'll help you develop both the skills and the self-marketing required to command the higher salaries.

Next, you won't spend your career at one company, and there's a special skill to finding and landing jobs. Most of us have learned this the hard way, after taking a few jobs that weren't a good match. Save yourself the trouble! Andy Lester teaches job-hunting skills in *Land the Tech Job You Love* [Les09].

Technical Lead

As you gain skill and experience—and increased salary—you will be expected to provide leadership as well. While leadership of the technical form doesn't come with the privilege of bossing people around, it *does* come with the privilege of bossing the product's design around.

Design is a separate skill than programming. The technical lead must work at both the big-picture level (seeing how the bricks fit together) and down at the guts level (building the bricks). Think of it as doing the *right thing* in the *right way*.

Of course, a product's design is merely a concept in people's minds; it's the manifestation of that concept—the code your team writes—that really counts. The second essential skill of a technical lead is shepherding a design as it is built. This isn't just documentation with pretty pictures at the front end of a project; it's hands-on writing code with people and making sure that the code develops over time toward the design and that the design evolves as project needs shift, too.

Management

If the technical lead role sounds like a bunch of responsibility with no authority, there's always management. Managers *do* get the privilege of bossing people around. (It doesn't work very well, but one can try.) Some programmers move into management because that's the only path upward in their company, and others genuinely have a talent for it.

That talent is a delicate balancing act between *leading* a team and *serving* the team. The leadership authority is pretty straightforward: people (mostly) do what the manager tells them to do. The service part, however, is just as important: the manager must match the work with the skills and interests of the workers, must provide them with equipment and training for both near-term goals and long-term growth, must fend for the team's budget and other resources, and must do much, much more.

If meetings and office politics drive you crazy, management is not your path. Much of a manager's work is accomplished in meetings: meetings with team members to make sure the right things are getting done the right way (aka *managing down*), meetings with superiors to ensure the team's work is aligning with the business needs (*managing up*), and meetings with peers to make sure the work is coordinated with the rest of the company (*managing across*).

Some managers attempt to also keep programming at the same time. I've never seen this work well; both their management work and their programming work get short-changed. Managing even a small team—and doing a good job at it—is a full-time job. Do one job or the other; don't try to do half of two jobs.

Product Management

While product management is in the domain of marketing (*egad!*), it's a natural transition for programmers who want to get into *what* products the company builds more than *how* the products are built. In fact, many product managers start their careers in engineering.

You probably have a gut feel for what your product should do. That's a good start. However, much like programming, the role of a product manager is part taste (aka gut feel) and part science. You'll need some education on marketing to fill in the latter half.

If your company attends trade shows or hosts conferences, that's a good opportunity to get out and talk with customers and the sales team. Try it. If you have fun, product management may be a path for you.

Academic Perspective: Graduate School

You should only look at graduate school for these reasons: you want a break from industry, you want to go into teaching, or you want to go into research. Your choice of school depends on your aim.

If you just want a break for a couple years and want to get a useful job credential, an MBA might be attractive. Here industry experience is extremely helpful. Be selective in choosing a school.

If you want to teach, any accredited PhD granting school will do. Here your industry experience will be very helpful to better understand researchable issues.

If your goal is major-league research, Carnegie Mellon, USC, Berkeley, and MIT are good places to start.

–David Olson, Department of Management, University of Nebraska

Academia

Some programmers will hit industry and decide they had a lot more fun in school. Teaching/research has its own pressures and rewards; if this is your gig, you can make a good living there. See David Olson's advice in *Academic Perspective: Graduate School*, on page 225.

Even for programmers who stay in industry, it's worth paying attention to research coming from academia—those underpaid and overworked grad students turn out some good ideas. Consider joining associations like ACM[7] and IEEE[8] to keep abreast of the latest research.

Actions

This tip isn't something you can act on today—ideally you're having a great time with programming. However, make a note to do a gut-check every year or so: do you enjoy the role you're in? Where do you see yourself going next? Is there any strategic-level learning or experience you can start on *now* to help you get there?

---

7. http://www.acm.org/
8. http://www.ieee.org/

Bibliography

[AS96]   Harold Abelson and Gerald Jay Sussman. *Structure and Interpretation of Computer Programs*. MIT Press, Cambridge, MA, 2nd, 1996.

[All02]   David Allen. *Getting Things Done: The Art of Stress-Free Productivity*. Penguin Group (USA) Incorporated, USA, 2002.

[Bec00]   Kent Beck. *Extreme Programming Explained: Embrace Change*. Addison-Wesley Longman, Reading, MA, 2000.

[Bec02]   Kent Beck. *Test Driven Development: By Example*. Addison-Wesley, Reading, MA, 2002.

[Bro95]   Frederick P. Brooks Jr.. *The Mythical Man Month: Essays on Software Engineering*. Addison-Wesley, Reading, MA, Anniversary, 1995.

[Bru02]   Kim B. Bruce. *Foundations of Object-Oriented Languages: Types and Semantics*. MIT Press, Cambridge, MA, 2002.

[CADH09]   David Chelimsky, Dave Astels, Zach Dennis, Aslak Hellesøy, Bryan Helmkamp, and Dan North. *The RSpec Book*. The Pragmatic Bookshelf, Raleigh, NC and Dallas, TX, 2009.

[FBBO99]   Martin Fowler, Kent Beck, John Brant, William Opdyke, and Don Roberts. *Refactoring: Improving the Design of Existing Code*. Addison-Wesley, Reading, MA, 1999.

[FP09]   Steve Freeman and Nat Pryce. *Growing Object-Oriented Software, Guided by Tests*. Addison-Wesley Longman, Reading, MA, 2009.

[Fea04]   Michael Feathers. *Working Effectively with Legacy Code*. Prentice Hall, Englewood Cliffs, NJ, 2004.

[Fow09]   Chad Fowler. *The Passionate Programmer: Creating a Remarkable Career in Software Development*. The Pragmatic Bookshelf, Raleigh, NC and Dallas, TX, 2nd, 2009.

[Fri89]   Robert Fritz. *The Path of Least Resistance: Learning to Become the Creative Force in Your Own Life*. Ballantine Books, New York, NY, USA, 1989.

[Gla02]   Malcolm Gladwell. *The Tipping Point: How Little Things Can Make a Big Difference*. Back Bay Books, New York, NY, USA, 2002.

[Gla06]   Malcolm Gladwell. *Blink*. Little, Brown and Company, New York, NY, USA, 2006.

[Gla08]   Malcolm Gladwell. *Outliers: The Story of Success*. Little, Brown and Company, New York, NY, USA, 2008.

[Gre10]   James W. Grenning. *Test Driven Development for Embedded C*. The Pragmatic Bookshelf, Raleigh, NC and Dallas, TX, 2010.

[Hun08]   Andrew Hunt. *Pragmatic Thinking and Learning: Refactor Your Wetware*. The Pragmatic Bookshelf, Raleigh, NC and Dallas, TX, 2008.

[KR98]   Brian W. Kernighan and Dennis Ritchie. *The C Programming Language*. Prentice Hall, Englewood Cliffs, NJ, Second, 1998.

[Kaw92]   Guy Kawasaki. *Selling the Dream*. Harper Paperbacks, New York, NY, USA, 1992.

[Les09]   Andy Lester. *Land the Tech Job You Love*. The Pragmatic Bookshelf, Raleigh, NC and Dallas, TX, 2009.

[Lio77]   John Lions. *Lions' Commentary on UNIX 6th Edition*. Peer-to-Peer Communications Inc., Charlottesville, VA, 1977.

[Mar08]   Robert C. Martin. *Clean Code: A Handbook of Agile Software Craftsmanship*. Prentice Hall, Englewood Cliffs, NJ, 2008.

[Mas06]   Mike Mason. *Pragmatic Version Control Using Subversion*. The Pragmatic Bookshelf, Raleigh, NC and Dallas, TX, 2006.

[Nö09]   Staffan Nöteberg. *Pomodoro Technique Illustrated: The Easy Way to Do More in Less Time*. The Pragmatic Bookshelf, Raleigh, NC and Dallas, TX, 2009.

[PP03]   Mary Poppendieck and Tom Poppendieck. *Lean Software Development: An Agile Toolkit for Software Development Managers*. Addison-Wesley, Reading, MA, 2003.

[Pie02]   Benjamin C. Pierce. *Types and Programming Languages*. MIT Press, Cambridge, MA, 2002.

[Ras10]   Jonathan Rasmusson. *The Agile Samurai: How Agile Masters Deliver Great Software*. The Pragmatic Bookshelf, Raleigh, NC and Dallas, TX, 2010.

[Rya10]   Terrence Ryan. *Driving Technical Change: Why People on Your Team Don't Act on Good Ideas, and How to Convince Them They Should*. The Pragmatic Bookshelf, Raleigh, NC and Dallas, TX, 2010.

[Sch04]   Ken Schwaber. *Agile Project Management with Scrum*. Microsoft Press, Redmond, WA, 2004.

[Ski97]   Steve S. Skiena. *The Algorithm Design Manual*. Springer, New York, NY, USA, 1997.

[Swi08]   Travis Swicegood. *Pragmatic Version Control Using Git*. The Pragmatic Bookshelf, Raleigh, NC and Dallas, TX, 2008.

[Tat10]   Bruce A. Tate. *Seven Languages in Seven Weeks: A Pragmatic Guide to Learning Programming Languages*. The Pragmatic Bookshelf, Raleigh, NC and Dallas, TX, 2010.

Index

Be Agile

Don't just "do" agile; you want to *be* agile. We'll show you how.

The best agile book isn't a book: *Agile in a Flash* is a unique deck of index cards that fit neatly in your pocket. You can tape them to the wall. Spread them out on your project table. Get stains on them over lunch. These cards are meant to be used, not just read.

Jeff Langr and Tim Ottinger
(110 pages) ISBN: 9781934356715. $15
http://pragprog.com/titles/olag

Here are three simple truths about software development:

1. You can't gather all the requirements up front. 2. The requirements you do gather will change. 3. There is always more to do than time and money will allow.

Those are the facts of life. But you can deal with those facts (and more) by becoming a fierce software-delivery professional, capable of dispatching the most dire of software projects and the toughest delivery schedules with ease and grace.

Jonathan Rasmusson
(280 pages) ISBN: 9781934356586.
$34.95
http://pragprog.com/titles/jtrap

Get Results

Reading about new techniques is one thing, making them work in your company and in the real world is another matter entirely. Here's the help you need.

If you work with people, you need this book. Learn to read co-workers' and users' *patterns of resistance* and dismantle their objections. With these techniques and strategies you can master the art of evangelizing and help your organization adopt your solutions.

Terrence Ryan
(200 pages) ISBN: 9781934356609.
$32.95
http://pragprog.com/titles/trevan

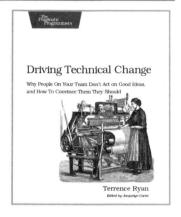

Technical Blogging is the first book to specifically teach programmers, technical people, and technically-oriented entrepreneurs how to become successful bloggers. There is no magic to successful blogging; with this book you'll learn the techniques to attract and keep a large audience of loyal, regular readers and leverage this popularity to achieve your goals.

Antonio Cangiano
(250 pages) ISBN: 9781934356883. $33
http://pragprog.com/titles/actb

The Pragmatic Bookshelf

The Pragmatic Bookshelf features books written by developers for developers. The titles continue the well-known Pragmatic Programmer style and continue to garner awards

Pragmatic Program-
top of your game.

us feedback, too!

nailing list, interact
rogrammers.

offerings.

this book entitles

nked, have color,
and iPod touch,

Write for Us: http://pragprog.com/write-for-us
Or Call: +1 800-699-7764